# Pediatric Brain Injury

## *A Practical Resource*

Carole Wedel Sellars, Ph.D., CCC-SLP
and
Candace Hill Vegter, M.A., CCC-SLP

Illustrations drawn under contract
by Annette Flaig

**Communication
Skill Builders**
3830 E. Bellevue/P.O. Box 42050
Tucson, Arizona 85733
(602) 323-7500

## Reproducing Pages from This Book

Many of the pages in this book can be reproduced for instructional or administrative use (not for resale). To protect your book, make a photocopy of each reproducible page. Then use that copy as a master for photocopying or other types of reproduction.

The following computer software products and peripheral equipment are cited in this book. These are included for illustrative purposes only; no endorsement is intended or should be inferred.

*Ace Reporter*™ and *Ace Inquirer*™ are trademarks of Methods & Solutions, Inc.

*Bankstreet Writer*®, *McGee*®, *McGee Visits Katie's Farm*®, *Where in the U.S.A. Is Carmen Sandiego?*®, and *Where in the World Is Carmen Sandiego?*® are trademarks of the Brøderbund Corporation.

ECHO® is a registered trademark of Street Electronics Corporation.

*Facemaker*™ and *Story Machine*™ are trademarks of Spinnaker Software.

*Factory*™, *Gears*™, *Iggy's Gnees*™, *Memory Building Blocks*™, *Memory Castle*™, *Royal Rules*™, *Teddy's Playground*™, and *What's in a Frame?*™ are trademarks of Sunburst/WINGS for Learning.

*Gertrude's Secrets*® and *Think Quick!*® are registered trademarks of The Learning Company.

IntroTalker™ is a trademark of Prentke Romich.

McCaw™ is a trademark of Zygo Industries.

Muppet Learning Keys™ is a trademark of Sunburst Communications.

*The Oregon Trail*™, *Word Munchers*™, and *Zoyon Patrol*™ are trademarks of Minnesota Education Computer Corporation.

PowerPad™ is a trademark of Dunamis, Inc.

SpeechViewer™ is a trademark of IBM.

*Stickybear*® *ABC*, *Stickybear*® *Opposites*, *Stickybear*® *Reading*, and *Stickybear*® *Shapes* are registered trademarks of Optimum Resource, Inc.

Speech Thing® is a registered trademark of Covox, Inc.

TouchWindow® is a registered trademark of Edmark Corp.

© 1993 by

**Communication Skill Builders, Inc.**

3830 E. Bellevue/P.O. Box 42050
Tucson, Arizona 85733
(602) 323-7500

ISBN 0-88450-643-6                    Catalog No. 7812

10 9 8 7 6 5 4 3 2
Printed in the United States of America

For information about our audio and/or video products, write us at: Communication Skill Builders, P.O. Box 42050, Tucson, AZ 85733.

# Dedication

*This book is enthusiastically dedicated to our children:*

*Jennifer*

*Alyssa*

*Micah*

*Amanda*

*because each accomplishment of theirs has repeatedly revealed the magic of becoming. This replenishes us as mothers and clinicians.*

*The reflection of learning in their faces underscores all children's drive to understand.*

*It is to that bountiful energy we dedicate our love and this book.*

# Amanda's Page

*And the youngest child, Amanda, age six, offered
to illustrate the book by drawing pictures
of children playing.*

*Thank you, Amanda.*

*And thank you, Annette, for the rest of the illustrations.*

# About the Authors

**Carole Sellars**, Ph.D, CCC-SLP, is the founder of the Pediatric Brain Injury Service at Gillette Children's Hospital in St. Paul, Minnesota. Currently she is the supervisor of speech pathology and the intake coordinator for the Brain Injury Service at Gillette Children's Hospital. She is a founding member of the Minnesota Head Injury Association, and Dr. Sellars has served on the MHIA board of directors. She received the B.S. degree from the University of Wisconsin, the M.S. degree in speech pathology from Florida State University, and a Ph.D. in health services from Walden University. She holds the Certificate of Clinical Competence from the American Speech Hearing Association.

**Candace Vegter**, M.A., CCC-SLP, is the program manager of the MINCEP® Epilepsy Care Program for Children at Gillette Children's Hospital, St. Paul, Minnesota. She received the B.A. degree in communication disorders from the University of Wisconsin and the M.A. degree in speech pathology from the University of Iowa. She also holds the Certificate of Clinical Competence from the American Speech-Hearing Association.

These authors have worked together for more than ten years, not only in the clinical setting but also presenting seminars and serving in professional associations. Together, they have worked on safety and prevention issues, conferences, and program development. They have also shared committee assignments on local, state, and national levels on specific issues of advocacy, program development, education, and prevention of injury.

They have been honored with the Elks Purple Cross, awarded in Alberta, Canada, given for their lectures on brain injury and children's safety issues.

# Acknowledgments

There have been many people who have silently contributed to this book. We wish to extend our gratitude to our professional colleagues, past and present, who have willingly shared their knowledge. The families and children with whom we have worked have added knowledge and an emotional base of experience from which we routinely draw. Thank you all. We would like specifically to acknowledge Joan and John Bergman and Linda King who contributed insightful and helpful additions to the chapter on the family.

On a family level, we would like to acknowledge our husbands, Stuart and John, for facilitating this endeavor with support, tolerance, and optimism. Having dedicated this book to our children, and as children ourselves, we would like to acknowledge our parents: Vicki Moen, Carole's mother; and Doc and Helen Hill, Candace's parents. Thank you for your confidence.

And finally we wish to acknowledge each other. This friendship of ours has defined encouragement. The collaborative effort of this book reflects our mutual respect, love, and care. It has been exhausting, fun, challenging, and spiritual to write it down.

Carole Wedel Sellars

Candace Hill Vegter

# Contents

## 14. Taking Care of You (While You're Taking Care of Others)

## 15. A Spiritual Look at a Career: What Recovering Children Have Taught Me

# Foreword

On several occasions we have been asked to write a book about children with brain injuries. Each time we declined, feeling we did not have a means to truly convey the essence of what we do. Videotapes of the children we work with have always been our best "illustrations." We were also hindered by the reservation that what we do is too spontaneous, too reactive to be put into step-by-step therapy procedures. But each time we presented a workshop or a conference, we have been further encouraged to "put it in writing."

So, here it is . . . not a cookbook, not a speech therapy manual, but everything we know and feel about dealing with children and adolescents: their injuries, their families, their education, and their future.

It has been challenging to determine our reading "audience." The primary audience is clinicians who have an interest in children with brain injuries. Additional and important audiences we had in mind while writing include families, teachers, and college students. We believe the application extends to those of you working with children with any etiology to a learning difference. We know it will not be new information to clinicians with extensive experience in pediatric brain injury.

We present this as a practical book written by seasoned clinicians for clinicians, educators, and families.

Carole Wedel Sellars

Candace Hill Vegter

# Introduction

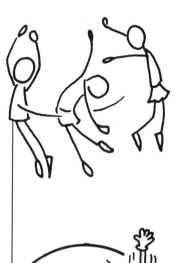

Children are verbs! They scoot, crawl, climb, walk, run, jump, skip, ride, play, swim, explore, and compete. They are motion with a smile. But children are not childproof. They can't have safety caps put on them. They fall out of windows, off of horses, and into swimming pools; they get hit by cars; they play with guns; they ride in many motorized vehicles; they ride on bikes, skateboards, and all-terrain vehicles; and they get hurt by adults.

This book is about children who get hurt and, more specifically, children who receive injuries to their brains. It is not about children who are injured before, during, or immediately after birth. It is about children who experience normalcy until a tragic accident interrupts their lives. These children will never be the same again.

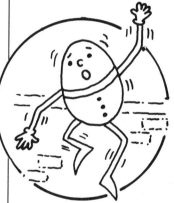

It is important to make the point at the very beginning that no matter how sophisticated the equipment or how well-trained the staff, these children simply cannot be put back together again. With very rare exceptions, they all have lost something in that accident. The point of this book is to present information to help families, clinicians, and educators maximize the child's recovery.

## Definition

Thankfully, body organs have an ability to withstand some injury or infection without any permanent damage. Cuts penetrate the skin, bones break, or surgery is done, and bodies heal. Similarly, most people have hit their heads with no resultant permanent damage other than a headache and scalp tenderness. This is in great credit to the protective skull.

Historically, significant brain injury has been associated with sustained loss of consciousness, but recent research (Boll 1983) has identified residual cognitive and behavioral deficits following minor head injury, sometimes with no loss of consciousness.

It is best from a purely practical level to view brain injury on a continuum of severity ranging from no loss of consciousness to death. There have been children who were never—or were only briefly—unconscious following their injury, but who experienced significant learning and behavioral problems many months later. However, most of the children have been unconscious for days, weeks, months, and in some cases, years.

**IMPORTANT**

**DEFINITION**

The definition used in this book is clinical and practical, but those who work with these children should recognize this definition as succinct and prognostic.

---

Brain Injury:

1. a sudden injury to the brain of a child

2. who has a history of normalcy

3. which results in a reduction in that child's ability to learn

---

For the purposes of this book, the history of normalcy can range from a few months in an infant to 17 years in a high school student. There have been some children, of course, who had learning disabilities or developmental delays prior to their brain injury, but the vast majority were normal until the accident.

# Incidence

It is sometimes helpful for families and clinicians to be aware of the incidence of brain injury in childhood. The magnitude of the problem is always impressive, and incidence figures stress the need for prevention, because even one child is too many.

In childhood and adolescence, accidents are the *leading cause of death and disability,* and the majority of these deaths and disabilities are due to brain injury (Lehr 1990).

Half of all deaths in childhood (ages 1 to 14) result from accidents (National Center for Health Statistics 1987). This figure is twice that of cancer and congenital defects combined.

Over one million children receive traumatic brain injuries each year (Lehr 1990). A more meaningful translation of these numbers might be:

- 66,666 Little League baseball teams; or

- 33,333 second-grade classes; or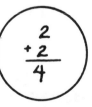

- 1,666 graduation classes from a large urban high school

**per year!**

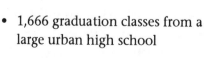

In recognition of the need for more accurate prevalence figures, the National Pediatric Trauma Registry was established in 1985 at the Department of Rehabilitation Medicine at Tufts University with a grant from the National Institute on Disability and Rehabilitation Research.

The objective was to create a database on multiple aspects of childhood trauma, including how children are injured, how their treatment is managed in the hospital, and the physical consequences of trauma to the child. The major emphasis is then to provide recommendations regarding the rehabilitative and preventive needs of injured children.

The following findings are based on the April, 1991, report on 13,321 injury cases:

- Boys are almost twice as likely as girls to be injured.

- Blunt trauma (closed head injuries) continue to be the most frequent injury affecting children.

- Penetrating injuries are increasing due to an increase in gunshot wounds.

- Falls are the most frequent cause of injury (26%).

- When traffic-related accidents are *combined* (motor vehicle occupant, pedestrian, motorcycle, bicycle, recreational vehicle), they account for 45% of all injuries.

- The majority of children (97%) survived their brain injury (NIDRR 1991).

# Categories of Injury

Children receive brain injuries in a variety of ways. Categorizing the types of injuries enhances parental education, team communication, and clinical intervention. The four categories include closed head injury, open head injury, anoxia, and infection.

## Closed Head Injury

The brain is not attached to the skull, and when the head hits or is hit by something, the brain moves around inside the skull. The skull remains intact, but the brain is damaged by the tearing and ripping of the cellular structures. In the same fashion, the brain bruises and bleeds inside the skull. The consistency of the brain is like gelatin, which makes it easier to understand how a blow to the skull can cause such extensive internal damage.

Damage occurs in both hemispheres of the brain. This damage may be seen as a collection of blood (hematoma) in one or several locations. If it is inside the brain, it is called an *intracerebral hematoma*. If it is between the brain and the membrane covering the brain, it is termed *subdural*. If

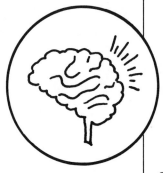

it is between the skull and the membrane covering the brain, it is termed *epidural*.

The increased blood in the brain causes swelling (edema). Because the brain is contained within the skull, the swelling is dangerous and may cause increased damage by constricting the brain. For this reason, medications are given to decrease swelling, and often an intracranial pressure monitor is placed in the brain to monitor pressure.

So often, families ask about where the injury is in the brain. A closed head injury often results in damage to both hemispheres, and though sophisticated diagnostic tests are used to determine the site of damage, the best indicator of damage location is what the child does or does not do clinically. (This will be discussed more fully in subsequent chapters.)

## Open Head Injury

In this form of brain injury, the skull is broken or penetrated. For example, the skull can fracture when the head hits the dashboard of the car; a bullet can pierce the skull; and the skull can be crushed by a kicking horse or the tire of a car. These open injuries result in bleeding and bruising inside the brain also, but sometimes the damage is contained more in one hemisphere.

## Anoxia

A severe brain injury can be caused by lack of oxygen, as is the case when children have respiratory and/or cardiac arrest in near-drowning accidents, choking, or status epilepticus, a constant seizing of the brain.

## Infection

Encephalitis and meningitis are occasional causes of brain injury in children. Encephalitis refers to swelling of the brain due to toxins, infection, or tumors. Meningitis refers to swelling of the coverings of the brain, the meninges. Sometimes meningo-encephalitis, a combination of the two, occurs.

Encephalitis is usually caused by a viral infection and meningitis by a bacterial infection. Immediate antibiotic treatment is very important. Sometimes these children have permanent brain damage from the swelling of the brain (Dodson and Alexander 1986).

Occasionally the different causes of brain injury occur at the same time. For example, a child may have a respiratory arrest after receiving a closed head injury.

**W**hat is the best way to think of brain injury?

With the exception of a penetrating injury such as a gunshot wound, the diffuse or spread-out damage seen in the vast majority of children ultimately results in a decrease in brain volume or mass. Over time, the primary injuries of bleeding, bruising, and swelling resolve and the remaining result is less brain mass. This is termed *atrophy* and is caused by enlarged lateral ventricles which decrease the amount of brain tissue.

This is the most functional, comprehensible way to view the result of brain injury: the brain tissue decreases in mass.

The next chapter describes in greater detail the anatomy and function of the brain to provide a reference point for the clinical interventions described.

# The Brain

## The Brain as a Whole: Command Central

Physiologically, the brain sits atop the rest of the body in a position of command, receiving, processing, organizing, and dispatching. It is considered to be the center of emotion, reasoning, creativity, thought, and intellect. It allows people to remember and to use past experiences to learn. Also important is the brain's role in monitoring other basic functions of the body, such as respiration, hunger, and thirst.

The brain is a complex, highly developed system that is vulnerable to injury and its sequelae at all levels of functioning. Many of these functions are so interrelated it is difficult to isolate specific sites of lesion that are responsible for observed differences. The nature of most brain injury results in diffuse lesions or numerous areas being affected, resulting in a conglomerate of behaviors rather than one predictable deficit.

This chapter is organized to cover basic structures of the brain and some of the expected sequelae of brain injury. It is intended as a refresher for professionals who have been separated from their neuroanatomy texts for a period of time, and as an introduction for professionals and families who have had limited exposure to children with brain injuries. The final portion of this chapter briefly covers diagnostic procedures, their acronyms, and their intended purpose.

## The Child's Brain

As with the other organs, the child's brain changes as it progresses through embryonic development. At birth, its basic structures are similar to the adult brain. A major difference, however, is that the brain tissue is about the consistency of custard until myelinization takes place.

Myelin acts as an insulator on the nerve and helps the transmission of nerve impulses. The progression of myelinization tells us about neurological development of the child's brain. The myelinization of the brain takes place during the first six to fifteen months of the child's development.

During this time, myelin is deposited along all the major fiber tracts, including those structures involved with recognition, emotions, bodily needs, and memory. The appearance and growth of myelin marks physiological development and allows for cognitive development to proceed.

The young brain requires sensory and motor experiences to promote and establish the networks and pathways throughout the brain. It is through these experiences that brain tissue is further assigned function. As these pathways develop, the brain becomes firmer. At the same time, as pathways become more firmly established, the brain becomes less *plastic,* referring to the young brain's capacity for reorganization if damage occurs early in development.

There is an important point to be made here. "Damage" in these cases refers to more localized events, such as a tumor or a stroke. In these types of cases, the brain is better able to reorganize and take over function from the affected areas than in cases where the trauma is more generalized. The diffuse damage that frequently occurs in severe traumatic brain injury has a significantly more profound effect on development.

Other differences between adult and child (such as the hardness of the skull and the size of the head in proportion to the body) are discussed further in Chapter 2, Children Are Not Little Adults.

# Injury: Its Impact and Implications

It is nearly impossible to describe all of the various results of traumatic brain injury because of the multi-focal nature of many of the injuries, the causes of the injury, and the age of the child. Certainly other factors, such as the child's pre-injury development and the home environment, play a significant role. It is important to stress, once again, that the sequelae of brain injury rarely are reflective of a localized injury; much more frequently, there has been diffuse injury that interrupts learning and alters development.

However, a basic understanding of the brain's responses to injury, as well as the anatomical relationship of the brain to the skull, may help to define some of the common characteristics noted in children with traumatic brain injury.

## Skull-Brain Interface

An obvious result of a blow to the head and brain is bleeding or hemorrhaging. The sites of blood collection (extradural hematoma, epidural hematoma, subdural hematoma, and intracerebral hematoma) are described in the introductory chapter of this book.

The important point to remember about bleeding is that the brain needs continued blood flow to function normally. As the blood collects, there is compression or distortion of the remaining structures of the brain. This compression increases the risk for loss of blood flow to other parts of the brain.

There are several injuries that are somewhat predictable because of the way the skull encases the brain:

- The bony surfaces near the frontal and temporal lobes are jagged. When the head is jarred or strikes an object, bruising of the brain is likely to occur in these areas.

- Severe injuries result when the brain twists on itself at the point where it connects to the brain stem. This area contains the nerve fibers that connect to the spinal column and send out signals to the muscles of the body.

- Injuries involving speed or high impact may result in a "coup/contre-coup" effect. When the head strikes an object, the brain then bounces against the opposite side of the skull, resulting in more than one area of damage and producing multi-focal deficits.

### Tissue Responses

One of the main patterns of injury is a more diffuse and nonspecific response to trauma. It results from the "shear-strain" effects that occur during rapid movement and impact (Jennett 1986). This rupturing and shearing of nerve fibers is referred to as diffuse axonal injury (DAI).

A second type of tissue damage results from interruptions in blood flow, referred to as ischemia.

Cerebral edema is brain swelling. It can be a focal or generalized response to injury to the brain. In the young child, this tends to happen very quickly and is sometimes referred to as "flash edema." Edema can cause secondary injuries as the swollen brain cells are pushed against the skull or against each other, resulting in reduced blood flow.

Keep in mind these typical responses of the brain to injury as you read the following description of the various structures of the brain, their roles, and how interference with their function affects the child's continued development.

# Structure of the Brain

### The Hemispheres—Right and Left

The two hemispheres of the brain appear to be identical in structure, although researchers have recently noted some subtle differences in size, with the "dominant" hemisphere appearing to be slightly larger. The dominant hemisphere is generally thought to contain the centers for speech and language. For most people, speech and language functioning

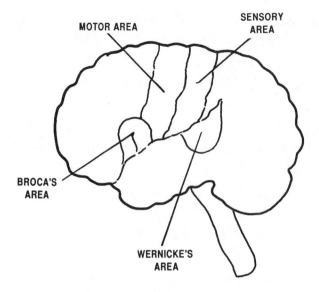

MOTOR AREA

SENSORY AREA

BROCA'S AREA

WERNICKE'S AREA

is contained in the left hemisphere, which also controls the right side of the body. This includes reception of sensory information as well as controlling the muscles.

Studies suggest that the right hemisphere of the brain influences the perception of visual and spatial information. For example, this perception is central to the ability to recognize facial expression and the subtleties of social situations. It seems to have great influence in the areas of judgment and monitoring of speech. It is also critical for recognition and use of intonation, recall of melody patterns, calculation, and construction.

Children with a left-sided weakness of the body typically demonstrate a flattened effect characterized by monotone speech and reduced facial expression. This is a clear example of the effects of right hemisphere involvement.

One should not think of the hemispheres functioning separately. Indeed, each hemisphere strongly influences the function of the other. For example, a child's language might be basically intact, but the child is unable to inhibit or monitor what is said in some social situations.

This is the child who classically sets out to tell about being hit while crossing the street and includes every detail down to the model year, color, and make of the car involved in the accident. In a group situation, this is the type of child who, when asked, "Can you tell Charlie why you're angry with him?" replies, "I hate his guts!"—end of discussion. These are children whose social language is clearly hindered by their right hemisphere lesions.

## The Lobes

The four lobes of the brain—frontal, parietal, temporal, occipital—are defined more by function than actual differences in the structure of the brain. Thus they are usually described according to landmarks in the brain.

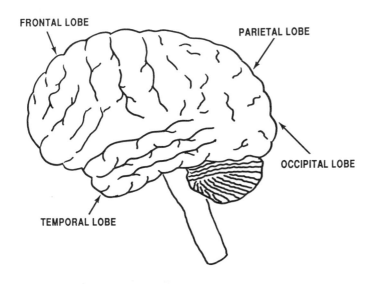

FRONTAL LOBE

PARIETAL LOBE

OCCIPITAL LOBE

TEMPORAL LOBE

## Frontal Lobes

The frontal lobes derive their name from their position in the brain. They occupy the most anterior (frontal) portion of the brain and contain about one-third of the surface of each hemisphere. The frontal lobes deal with matters of intellect and planning (Gilling and Brightwell 1982).

These lobes receive information (including memories of past experiences) from other parts of the brain, and assist in making decisions about what to do. In the current literature this is frequently referred to as *executive functioning,* that is, the ability to exercise judgment based on incoming information.

A cautionary note must be inserted here. Executive functioning is heavily dependent on a wealth of past experiences and consequences—experiences not encountered by the young child. It is a term more appropriately used with older children and adults. To keep expectations in perspective, executive functioning must be measured against the child's developmental level. Three-year-olds make pretty poor executives!

Injuries to the frontal lobe commonly exacerbate the young child's already impulsive behavior and interrupt the development of higher cognitive abilities. Children with such injuries can be very distractible, acting on everything they see or hear.

The frontal lobes contain the motor strips for the opposite side of the body. These strips control large and small muscle movement for all physical activity, such as running, throwing, singing, and eating. Injuries to the left motor strip will result in muscle involvement of the right side of the body, while injury to the right motor strip will be reflected in motor weakness or paralysis on the left side of the body. This includes not only the muscles for the trunk and body, but muscles for chewing, swallowing, speech, and facial effect.

Broca's area is located in the left frontal area just adjacent to the motor strip. Speech-language pathologists are well aware of the resulting speech deficits secondary to an injury to this area. A child typically will struggle with the initiation and planned movement of speech. This is termed *verbal apraxia* and is discussed in Chapter 8, The Structure-Dependent Child.

A child who has gone over the handlebars of a bike and landed head-first will frequently demonstrate a rather severe apraxia of speech during the first days or weeks of recovery. This seems to be the result of edema in the frontal lobes, resulting in compression of Broca's area. Generally, this type of apraxia resolves in a relatively short period of time as the edema diminishes.

### Parietal Lobes

Lying posterior to the frontal lobes are the parietal lobes. They receive incoming sensory information from skin, muscles, tendons, and joints, then coordinate this with incoming data from auditory and visual centers to convey information about the body's position in space and how the body is moving. The parietal lobes influence the messages that are sent to the motor areas.

Anyone who has watched a young child's first attempts to draw a circle or triangle or perform a somersault can understand that the parietal areas, too, are involved in a developmental process. The younger the child at the time of injury, the less well established are these skills.

> Injury to the right and left parietal lobes results in different types of behaviors.
>
> With injury on the left, typical behaviors include difficulty in drawing, copying, dressing, differentiating right from left, and problems with some arithmetic calculations.

Children with right parietal involvement display more severe difficulty in copying designs, also showing a tendency to omit the left side of their drawings and to neglect the left side of their bodies and environment. They tend to have difficulty recognizing familiar faces. Children may be confused with steps that require sequencing, such as dressing. They have difficulty with time and space and may get lost easily.

### Temporal Lobes

Running laterally on either side of the brain are the temporal lobes. They are central to memory functioning. The hippocampus and amygdala lie within the temporal lobe and are described later in this chapter. The hippocampus and part of the temporal lobe are important players in recent memory storage.

The temporal lobes are also implicated in some emotional responses through the limbic system. Using past experiences, the temporal lobes

*In their confusion, some children have insisted that we are their aunts or, worse yet, their grandmothers.*

help in distinguishing what is acceptable or "good for us" from something that is not acceptable or "bad."

Auditory information is processed in the left posterior temporal lobe known as Wernicke's area.

Unfortunately, the location of the temporal lobes within the skull places them at high risk for injury.

A child with injury to Wernicke's area may appear confused by language. In fact, the use of language may increase agitation in some of these children. Their own language may contain jargon or words that do not make sense.

Damage to the right temporal lobe can result in the incessant speech described earlier.

Injuries to the temporal lobes also seem to be implicated in reduced ability to recognize the surrounding situation and evaluate safety or danger issues. For example, by the time children are 5 years old, they have developed some judgment around heights because they have had experiences with falling and hurting themselves.

When children who have developed this judgment stand on the edge of a high structure such as a slide, they look to see how far they would fall if they jumped. Based on all the information—what they see, their past experiences with jumping, and their levels of judgment and impulse control—they make the decision whether or not to launch off the top of the ladder.

Contrast this behavior with a child who has sustained an injury to the frontal and temporal lobes of the brain. This child is much more likely to stand on the bed, see an opportunity to jump, have no recognition of impaired movement and coordination, and possess little recall of the consequences of falling. That child is much more likely to hurdle impulsively into space, much to the horror of parents and primary nurses. In many cases, explanations and reprimands have little impact, because the child is unable to store this information for future reference. This situation causes a lot of premature graying for clinicians!

Chapter 8, describing the structure-dependent child, discusses this issue further.

### Occipital Lobes

The occipital lobes are located at the posterior end of the cortex. They have the extremely important role of receiving and interpreting visual information. Once received, this information is sent anteriorly through various relay stations, ultimately arriving in the frontal lobes to be processed with other information.

Because of its small size, injury to the occipital lobe can have a profound impact. A phenomenon called *visual agnosia* may result in the child's being able to "see" an object but unable to "recognize" it.

Cortical blindness is a symptom of severe damage to the occipital area. In some, this condition is transitory. There are children who have remained functionally blind for weeks and months, then almost miraculously begin to evidence vision. What these children initially perceive is often confused or distorted but, over time, their interpretation of visual information gradually improves.

The optic tract courses from the eyes to the occipital lobe in the posterior portion of the brain. Damage along the visual pathways results in field cuts or defects. Depending on the location of the lesion, the child's vision is characterized by a visual image that contains only part of what is actually being seen. For example, a child may see only the left side of a page or the right side of someone's face.

Children learn to accommodate for this visual defect through practice and adaptations to printed materials. In the initial period of recovery, however, while the child is quite confused, it may be very difficult to sort out the type and extent of the visual impairments.

Damage to the cranial nerves that innervate the extraocular muscles can result in diplopia or double vision. This is frequently treated with eye patches.

## Association Areas

While each of the four lobes has predisposed abilities, none of them functions solely or adequately without information from other parts of the brain. Each lobe transmits and receives information. Loss of even small portions of information results in distorted or inaccurate perceptions.

Integration, interpretation, and adjustment occur continuously throughout the cortical areas via the association areas. These are connected by association fibers which allow the various areas of the brain to communicate with each other. Connections run between the right and left hemispheres and parts of the same hemisphere.

## Cerebellum

The cerebellum is sometimes called the "little brain." It is located at the base of the brain, beneath the cerebral hemispheres and behind the brain stem. Its primary function is to coordinate the fine muscular movements that have been initiated by other areas of the brain. Studies suggest that some overlearned responses may be stored in the cerebellum.

Injury to the cerebellum can result in changes in fine motor movement, balance, posture, and coordination. Children with ataxic movements reflect injury to the cerebellum. The child who falls backward off a swing—or out of a pickup—may reflect cerebellar injuries.

## Limbic System

There are "inner" structures of the brain that are very involved in emotion, attention, memory, and learning. These include the amygdala and the hippocampus in the temporal lobe, and the thalamus and hypothalamus above the midbrain area. These four bodies are referred to as the limbic system. They form a composite structure that regulates emotional state, perception, attitude, and motivation.

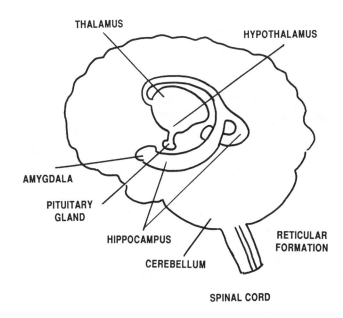

The amygdala is involved with emotional responses such as fear and aggression. It is vital in one's ability to respond quickly to an emergency.

The hippocampus, located within the temporal lobe, is strongly implicated in learning and memory.

The thalamus is located above the midbrain and functions as the great relay station. It receives sensory input and dispatches information to the cortex and hypothalamus.

The hypothalamus regulates appetite, thirst, body temperature, and secretions of the pituitary gland. Children with injury to this area may demonstrate insatiable appetites resulting in excessive weight gain. All too often, children with such injuries have been observed to jeopardize their physical recovery because of the drive to eat and their inability to modify their eating patterns.

Because of their location within the temporal lobe, the structures of the limbic system are vulnerable to injury. As a result, children with damage to this area will typically demonstrate difficulty in sorting relevant incoming sensory information from irrelevant information. Their concentration and attention, as well as emotional responses, are impaired. Because they cannot always focus on the important parts of new information, memory storage and recall are diminished.

This interruption in normal learning patterns presents major challenges to parents, educators, and therapists. Further discussion of cognitive sequelae is covered in Chapter 8, The Structure-Dependent Child, and Chapter 9, The Concrete Processor.

## Brain Stem

While high value is placed on intellect and emotion, the part of the brain that is the most vital to survival is the most primitive part of the brain, the brain stem. This is the structure through which the cerebral hemispheres send and receive signals to and from the spinal cord and the peripheral nervous system.

Deep within the brain stem is the reticular formation. It is influential in arousal, consciousness, drowsiness, and attention. Also within the brain stem are the centers which control breathing, heart rate, and blood pressure. Because the reticular formation is so heavily involved with the level of consciousness, damage to this area can result in prolonged coma.

## Cranial Nerves

Within the brain stem and the midbrain are the motor and sensory nuclei of the cranial nerves. These nerves relay peripheral motor and sensory information to and from the muscles of the head and neck. They are vital to the senses of smell, taste, hearing, and vision, and control the muscles of the eyes, face, neck, tongue, heart, lungs, palate, pharynx, larynx, trachea, and gastrointestinal tract.

| Nerve | Name | Function |
|-------|------|----------|
| I | Olfactory | Perception of smell |
| II | Optic | Reception of visual information |
| III | Oculomotor | In conjunction with IV and VI, controls the muscles of the eyes |
| IV | Trochlear | Superior oblique muscle of the eye |
| V | Trigeminal | Sensation of the face; muscles involved in chewing |
| VI | Abducens | Lateral rectus muscle of the eye |
| VII | Facial | Sensory for the tongue and palate; motor to the muscles of the face |
| VIII | Vestibulocochlear | Reception of auditory signals; influences balance and equilibrium |
| IX | Glossopharyngeal | Sensation of the posterior portion of the tongue and pharynx; muscles of the pharynx |
| X | Vagus | Motor and sensory to heart, lungs, palate, pharynx, larynx, trachea, lungs, and stomach |
| XI | Accessory | Muscles of the neck |
| XII | Hypoglossal | Muscles of the tongue |

(Taken from Netter 1989)

Children with cranial nerve injuries will potentially have difficulties with speech, eating, facial affect, vision, hearing, and motion sickness.

# Alphabet Soup: Diagnostic Tests

The hospital staff tends to talk in "alphabet soup"—PT, PM and R, WHO, AFO, and so forth. The following descriptions provide basic explanations of those tests that are used in assessing the brain's status. The list is not inclusive but covers the more commonly used procedures.

## EEG

*EEG* stands for *electroencephalogram*. Small electrodes are temporarily glued to the scalp and detect the electrical activity of the brain. The electrical signals are recorded as a graphlike representation of brain wave patterns. This information is helpful in showing whether there is seizure activity. Other abnormal patterns (such as "slowing") can also tell the neurologist something about the extent and location of brain damage.

## MRI

*MRI—magnetic resonance imaging*—is a way to examine the structure of the brain. The MRI measures tissues of varying density in the brain by bombarding the brain with harmless magnetic fields. It detects large and small changes in the brain, such as a tumor or hemorrhage. This information may be helpful in determining the extent and the site of a lesion.

## CT or CAT

*Computerized axial tomography* uses X-ray and computer technology to reconstruct brain shadows as precise, three-dimensional images. This produces a picture of the internal structures of the brain.

## PET

While the MRI and the CT deal with structures, the *PET (positron emission tomography)* reveals some information about the function of the various structures of the brain. Scientists know that glucose is absorbed by the active portions of the brain. The patient is given radioactive glucose and then asked to perform a variety of activities. The PET scanner can trace the location of such activities as motor movement, speech, and vision. Damaged areas show decreased glucose uptake.

All of these procedures provide some information as to the extent of injury and result of the injury. They do not, however, reveal everything about function or outcome. That information is obtained through observation and interaction with the child over long periods of time. (Predictors of outcome are discussed in Chapter 12 on research findings.)

● ● ● ● ●

This has been a very simplified approach to an extremely complex system. The brain has revealed only a few of its many mysteries despite centuries of medical, scientific, and psychological investigation.

The important point to remember as you wade through this material is that rarely does a child who sustains a significant brain injury evidence a localized injury. Most demonstrate generalized injuries in addition to localized insults. Any disruption of the brain that interferes with the ability of the brain to communicate with all of its parts presents an interruption to the child's development. This results in changes in cognitive, motor, emotional, and perceptual skills that will be described in more detail in Chapters 7, 8, and 9 dealing with the four levels of consciousness.

# Children Are Not Little Adults

To most, the title of this chapter is probably self-explanatory. Any parent understands that a child does not reason as an adult. Any teacher will verify that a child's attention is not that of an adult's. But as pediatric programs for traumatic brain injury have been initiated, there has been a tendency to impose adult models of rehabilitation, probably because adult rehabilitation programs existed long before rehabilitation programs began to examine the needs of children.

It is important to tear down or at least partially rearrange those adult-based structures to better accommodate the needs of the child and the family. To rebuild a children's rehabilitation program successfully, the *child* needs to be viewed as the foundation, with the following areas given careful consideration:

- neuropathology of brain injury in children

- normal development and its implications in recovery

- application of principles of child-centered care

## Neuropathology of Brain Injury in Children

From birth to age 2, the child's brain is particularly vulnerable to injury. At birth, the cranial vault is pliable, composed of floating plates. The skull does not become solid and rigid until 1 year of age, and the anterior fontanel may not ossify or harden completely until 2 years of age.

Several studies refer to poorer outcomes for children under 2 years of age, possibly related to the following factors:

- The immature brain has not completed its myelinization process. The softer consistency is more susceptible to injury when the head is jarred.

- There is reduced ability for the brain of the young child to self-regulate swelling following injury. This is referred to as *flash edema* and results in secondary injuries as the swollen brain presses against the skull.

To illustrate the difference between the mature brain and the young child's brain, one neurologist has described injury to the adult brain as shaking a bowl of gelatin, while injury to a child's brain is similar to shaking a bowl of custard.

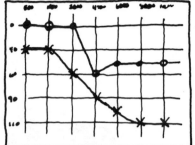

Hearing loss is a concern in children with brain injuries. In one program in Canada, 7% of the children admitted had temporal bone fractures. As a result of this type of injury, sensorineural hearing loss was noted in 13% of the children. A conductive loss (having to do with the ear drum and bones of the ear) was noted for 24% of the children. This underscores the importance of hearing screening for all children admitted with head trauma.

Early seizures, defined as those occurring in the first four weeks of injury, appear to be more prevalent in children than adults. Status epilepticus (prolonged seizure activity) occurs more frequently in children. For this reason, it is extremely important that a pediatric neurologist monitor the child's neurological status, order video EEGs, and, if necessary, prescribe anti-epileptic medications. Some medications cause side effects, and it is important to look for signs of drowsiness, hyperactivity, changes in appetite, balance difficulties, and irritability.

Earlier researchers placed a good deal of faith in the plasticity of the brain and proposed that children have a better prognosis for recovery than adults. However, if brain injury is defined as an interruption of normal development, the outcome is sometimes negatively influenced by the age of the child: the younger the child, the greater the chance of affecting the child's development.

The stages of normal development are described below, along with a discussion of how interruption at those stages might influence outcome.

## Implications of Normal Development in Recovery

### Birth to 3 Years

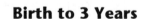

It is obvious that rapid changes take place in the first three years of life. The child progresses from a completely dependent creature to one that walks, talks, and independently raids the cupboards and refrigerator. The amount of learning that takes place is phenomenal. But if a defective cognitive system is interposed—one that includes attention, memory, and judgment difficulties—the effects on learning are numerous.

Additionally, because of the anatomical differences described previously, the young child is more likely to experience generalized brain insults rather than focal lesions. Even minor head injury may result in diffuse and generalized impairment in the younger child. This is generally more devastating to the development of higher cognitive functions (Boll 1983).

Compounding these cognitive differences is the fact that younger children may have communication and physical differences that interfere with independent exploration of their environment. This, too, can have a negative effect on the progression of normal development.

Many developmental theorists are disputing Piaget's levels of development. The general feeling is that these levels are not static but are interdependent. Nevertheless, Piaget's descriptions of observed behaviors at various levels help adults to view the world through the child's eyes and to understand how children think.

## Preoperational Level

Until about the age of 7 or so, children function at what Piaget has described as the preoperational level of thinking. Information needs to be in meaningful context. Children have limited ability to visualize or understand something that is unknown to them.

Children use language in a very concrete fashion. A favorite example of this is the 3-year-old who was asked by her father to "please not shout at the table." The 3-year-old shouted in irritation, "I'm **not** shouting at the **table,** I'm shouting at **you!**"

Throughout this level of development, vocabulary acquisition is ongoing. A strong foundation of vocabulary comprehension and usage is the basis for later abstract thinking and verbal expression.

During these years, children began to comprehend how the world around them works—how things are alike, and how things are different. They begin to look at objects as not just a whole, and can begin to describe qualities, parts, function, and so on.

Interruptions in learning at any point can have profound effects on the child's ability to develop later abstract thinking skills.

## Concrete Operations

From ages 7 to 12, children begin to demonstrate the ability to exercise abstract thought. During this period, children's use and perception of language is expanding and allowing for increased abstract thought. Their thinking is more flexible, and they can look at new information from several different angles. Their recognition of humor reflects awareness of puns and plays on words.

These are the precursors to being able to predict consequences, to function beyond the here and now. If the child's learning is hindered or interrupted, the child tends to be unable to move into the higher levels of thinking that permit functioning in the adult world.

## Abstract Thinking

By age 12 and up, the child is demonstrating established concepts of space and time. While still somewhat immature in the approaches to problem solving and judgment issues, the older child at least has had some life experiences and overlearned information that provide some type of anchor during the phases of life recovery.

However, the lack of social maturation can have its effects. A study conducted at the University of Maryland School of Medicine found that the normal developmental stages of adolescence are significantly complicated by the presence of even minor brain injuries (Jacobson et al. 1986).

# Application of Principles in Child-Centered Care

*"Pediatrics" refers to birth through 18 years of age. This covers a tremendous range of behavior, cognitive, and physical development, and we cannot presume to cover all the needs of this group. That is better left to developmental psychologists. However, we would like to offer some general "hints from hindsight," from the "if I had it to do over again" category.*

- *Don't expect any more from a hospitalized child than you would expect from any other child. We often reflect that our own children would not tolerate uncomfortable exercises or the constant demands of strangers. These children are frightened, anxious of strangers, and confused by what is happening to them.*

- *Parents are the center of the child's universe. It is important to allow parents to remain with their children. It establishes trust with the child and is the basis for the parents to begin to trust you as a therapist. (There will be more about this in Chapter 5 on the family.)*

- *Hospital is not home. No matter how wonderful we are and how nice our facilities, we cannot reproduce home. There are some things we can do, however, to narrow the distance a little between hospital and home. Dress children in their own clothes. Ask family members to bring children's blankets and teddy bears, then use these beloved objects as part of their therapy. Encourage parents and children to individualize their rooms with their belongings.*

- *Materials must have an appeal to the child. We have many discussions as to what defines "age-appropriate" activities. For example, a worksheet that may be "age appropriate" for a 10-year-old is not likely to hold a child's attention in the early stages of recovery.*

We prefer to select materials and activities that are appropriate to the child's current level of cognitive functioning. This may mean the use of a preschool computer program for a 12-year-old. Most families accept this if you explain your rationale, the goal you are trying to achieve, and that the level of difficulty will be increased as the child progresses.

- Power struggles are a waste of time and energy. Keep in mind that you are dealing with children who have limited reasoning abilities and poor insights. Try restructuring an activity or switching activities if the child does not seem to be able to cooperate. It's okay to rock or comfort a child during therapy. Therapy is a learning experience. It should be positive.

- Children are naturally egocentric. It is an important part of their development. They have trouble seeing beyond their immediate needs. If you expect this, it is less likely to "getcha."

- Don't impose adult standards of socially acceptable behavior on children. They have their own rules of operation. Most children have no social investment in paying attention to your goals or your lesson plan. What you are doing and planning must have immediate meaning and a payoff for them.

- Children nap. Just because children are in the hospital does not mean they can function without their normal naps and rest periods. Few parents attempt to take a toddler anywhere when it is nap time. Children recovering from brain injuries and accompanying infections frequently need more rest time than we generally allow. It is important for the staff to work with the family to schedule quiet times away from activity. As recovery progresses, goals for increased endurance can be implemented.

- Children need room to zoom—advice from the Pediatric Center at Rancho Los Amigos. A pediatric hospital requires indoor and outdoor play space that is safe for children. A supervised pool time is critical, as are outings and weekend passes.

- The young child has no concept of time—what ten minutes means, what a week means, what a month is. Yet we have a tendency to expect them to understand when we explain that the pain will last only "a few more minutes" or that mom will be here "in the evening."

  As much as possible, it is essential to put time measurements in simple and familiar terms. The child life specialist works with calendars to mark off days until a weekend pass. We set timers or mark activities on a paper to show how much has been completed and what remains to be done. We talk about the weather and holidays rather than expecting the child to know a particular month.

- *Children basically want to adore the adults in their life. Don't betray that trust. Reassure them that they are good kids even if you have to do it through clenched teeth. They thrive on your praise and are vulnerable to your disapproval.*

  *If you have to curtail a behavior, direct your criticism toward the behavior or the action, not the child. For example, "It is dangerous to throw things" is much more constructive than "That was a naughty thing you did."*

  *Children's joy is contagious—certainly one thing worth catching from them.*

- *Learn from the children. Their behaviors are the best barometers as to how they are feeling and responding. When things are not going as expected, back off for a moment and re-evaluate. Look at the situation through the child's eyes. It may open your own.*

● ● ● ● ●

Children take on the world in a simple and direct fashion; to effectively maximize a child's recovery, the child must be treated as a child. In the following chapters that deal with the levels of consciousness, it will be important to remember that the principles of therapy are based on the child's development and the impact of interruptions in that development.

# Assessment: Levels of Consciousness

It is important to have a measurement, an evaluative yardstick, to measure a child's progress, provide information for families, and facilitate team communication. This chapter explains the concept of levels, or stages, of consciousness. The chapter also describes two prominent adult scales for assessing recovery from brain injury and presents a pediatric scale that has been very useful.

## The Language of Coma

A person on television experiences a brain injury and lies in a hospital bed with only one discreet oxygen tube in the nose obstructing an otherwise unmarred face. The person "wakes up" weeks later, generally with a startled expression and a completely intelligible sentence—"Geez, gosh, where am I? What am I doing in this hospital bed?" The person recognizes everyone immediately, the family breathes a collective sigh of relief, and life goes on exactly as before.

Wouldn't that be nice? But of course the *reality* of coma doesn't look pretty: tracheostomies, ventilators, nasogastric tubes, suctioning devices, intracranial pressure monitors, catheters, shaved heads, and intravenous drips. Sometimes the child is unrecognizable because of facial bruising and swelling.

There are many ways to describe coma—*coma, stupor, vegetative state, unconsciousness*—and this only adds to the family's confusion.

It is more helpful to describe a child's recovery behaviorally because the family knows where the child is currently functioning and what to hope for next. A behavioral scale also underscores the reality that recovery from brain injury is a process—it doesn't just happen magically as on television.

# Adult Scales

## Glascow Coma Scale

The Glascow Coma Scale is used to evaluate and quantify observation of a person with a brain injury. Developed by Teasdale and Jennett (1974), this useful scale defines coma as (1) the absence of eye opening, (2) the inability to obey commands, and (3) the inability to speak recognizable words.

The lowest score on this scale is 3 and the highest score is 15. Generally a person is assessed on this scale numerous times across a hospital stay to record progress.

**Eye Opening**

| | |
|---|---|
| spontaneous | 4 |
| to speech | 3 |
| to pain | 2 |
| none | 1 |

**Best Motor Response**

| | |
|---|---|
| obeys commands | 6 |
| localizes | 5 |
| withdraws | 4 |
| abnormal flexion | 3 |
| extensor response | 2 |
| none | 1 |

**Verbal Response**

| | |
|---|---|
| oriented | 5 |
| confused conversation | 4 |
| inappropriate words | 3 |
| incomprehensible sounds | 2 |
| none | 1 |

(Teasdale and Jennett 1974, 81-84).

Mild brain injury corresponds to a total score of 13 to 15. This could be an adult who opens eyes to speech (3), obeys a few commands (6), and speaks in confused sentences (4).

A moderate injury scores between 9 and 12. This could be an adult who opens eyes to speech (3), localizes touch and movement (5), and says a few inappropriate words (3).

A severe injury corresponds to a score from 3 to 8. This could be a person who opens eyes to pain (2), has arms and legs that are extended with high muscle tone (2), and makes a few incomprehensible sounds (2).

## Levels of Cognitive Functioning (Rancho Scale)

Traditionally, the Glascow Coma Scale is used in the emergency room and during early acute care to evaluate neurological status and progress. Another scale that is used extensively in the rehabilitation phase of recovery is termed the "Rancho Scale" because it was developed by professionals in brain injury rehabilitation at Rancho Los Amigos Hospital, Downey, California. This scale is more descriptive in nature and measures cognitive rather than physical recovery.

I. No response to stimulation

II. Generalized response to stimulation

III. Localized response to stimulation

IV. Confused, agitated behavior

V. Confused, inappropriate, nonagitated behavior

VI. Confused, appropriate behavior

VII. Automatic, appropriate behavior

VIII. Purposeful, appropriate behavior

(Taken from *Rehabilitation of the head injured adult: Comprehensive physical management,* 1979, Rancho Los Amigos Hospital, Downey, California)

This scale has been used so often in adult rehabilitation that when professionals describe a person as "Level 5," everyone on the team knows what behaviors the patient exhibits.

Unfortunately there is no such popular, widely used scale for children. There are many reasons for this. Adult scales evaluate a person's forms of speech responses, but if the child is an infant, this obviously is not appropriate. Additionally, children do not seem to pass routinely or predictably through periods of agitation as often as adults.

# A Practical Pediatric Scale

To reiterate, it is very useful to have a yardstick to evaluate progress. A pediatric scale was developed by the professionals at Rancho Los Amigos Hospital. An adapted version of this scale is included in Appendix A as a reproducible form.

## The Pediatric Brain Injury Scale
### (adapted from the Rancho Los Amigos Pediatric Scale)

**Level 5:** No response to sensory stimuli, including pain. This is often the status of the child in the emergency room.

**Level 4:** A generalized response to sensory stimuli. Children blink their eyes to very loud sound and generally grimace to light touch with a feather on the face. Often these children blink to protect their eyes when a toy or hand is passed quickly before their eyes (visual threat).

**Level 3:** A localized response. At this level children turn to find the sound or voice and often push people away or pull on their tubes. They can follow objects and people with their eyes, and some children begin to smile at this level.

**Level 2:** At this stage, children are no longer in a coma. They are *consistently* able to follow verbal commands or gestured requests such as "Give it to me; don't touch; touch your nose; point to daddy." They participate in therapy by doing simple puzzles, imitative play, and early academic and attention programs on a computer. They often smile and laugh aloud, and some begin to feed themselves and wheel a wheelchair. Many children begin to speak at this level.

**Level 1:** At this stage children are oriented and can state where they are and what has happened to them, and recall events that happened an hour ago or a day ago. Many children are walking independently and talking in complete sentences at this level. Remaining deficits usually exist in processing abstract information, impulse control, balance, organization, and visual perception.

**Level 0:** At this level, children are *exactly* as they were before their accident.

---

In many years of working with children with brain injuries, only a very few children, out of hundreds, have been observed to return to their pre-accident status, and these children had only momentary loss of consciousness. Sometimes the remaining deficits are subtle (such as difficulty organizing school work, impulsivity, or impaired balance), but the deficits are there. Thus, most of the children are usually discharged at Level 1.

# Assessing the Child on the Pediatric Scale

The magic word in assessment is *consistency*. The child must do the items at that level for everyone—parents, nurses, doctors, and therapists. The child must be able to do the behaviors at 8 in the morning and 3 in the afternoon for Uncle Harry or Doctor Wedel.

The obvious question is how to evaluate a 10-month-old child with respect to orientation and following commands? Please refer to Appendix A for a checklist with which to evaluate children on these levels in three categories: 6 months to 2 years, 2 to 5 years, and school age.

This scale is appropriate for children with closed or open head injuries described previously. It is not nearly as helpful or developmentally appropriate for children whose brain injury results from an anoxic or infectious cause, because the mechanism of injury and prognosis differ in anoxic and infectious injuries.

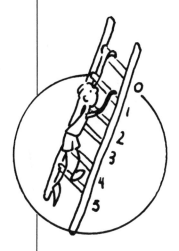

Categorizing recovery into these levels helps families understand that recovery from brain injury is a long process. These divisions also help hospital team members communicate with a child. But the levels are not like steps on a ladder, with every child reaching the top. Some children never get better than Level 4. Some spend four months at Level 2 before going to Level 1, some go from Level 4 to 1 in one week, and some go from 2 to 3 in a half-hour therapy session. They do reflect progress, however, and with the exception of extreme fatigue or a brief bout with an illness, the children move **forward**. We have never known a child to reach Level 2 and then go back to Level 4. And that, in a nutshell, is why we have worked so long with children with brain injuries: **they keep getting better!**

# All the King's Horses and . . . The Team

The word *team* conjures up images of a group of individuals with similar backgrounds, training, and philosophy charging forward on a playing field of some sort—carrying out the game plan, blocking for each other, passing the ball off if one individual falls short of the goal. Ultimately, with one last surge, the ball is carried over the goal, and the crowd cheers madly.

Ideally, that is the way teams should function. All members should have a common goal and a plan, and all members should contribute equally in their efforts. Reality, however, is that fumbles occur, plays are changed at the line of scrimmage, or the unexpected happens and the opposing forces come crashing through the line.

The recovery of child and family following a brain injury requires so many team members that the formulation and implementation of a rehabilitation plan is very complicated indeed.

## An Integrated Approach to a Complicated Problem

Anyone who has worked in the area of pediatric rehabilitation for traumatic brain injury will tell you that the team has to put forth an integrated effort. In practice, this means that all individuals must be familiar with the cognitive, physical, and psychosocial needs of the child.

The group must define individual responsibilities but also must acknowledge the need for overlap and redundancy of activities. This is particularly true in the area of cognitive retraining.

*In our program, all the professionals as well as the family are considered cognitive retrainers. For example, it is inappropriate to teach children to walk if you are not at the same time teaching them how to find their way back to their room.*

## Communication

One of the key components in team functioning is communication. The group must speak the same jargon or lingo. That should not imply complicated or foreign terminology but rather commonality of language. This is one of the primary reasons for the use of scales of recovery. When discussing the child at Level 1, for example, the use of that description encompasses a composite of behaviors that should be familiar to all team members.

Team members must communicate on a regularly scheduled basis, among themselves as well as with the family. This is accomplished through written goals as well as staff conferences.

Formally, each team member writes a weekly summary that is shared verbally at a staffing conference. Rationale and modifications of goals are discussed at that time. Questions that have been raised by the family or school are shared and further goals are established.

The staff also meets with the family on a formal basis every two or three weeks. (The format for those meetings, along with written goals, are discussed further in Chapter 5, The Family.)

The communication that takes place on a daily basis among the professionals involved in caring for and working with the child is of utmost importance.

- While readying the child for transport, the nurse tells the aide that Tina is sad this morning because her sister is sick and her mom cannot be at the hospital today. This is important information to share with the therapists and may account for Tina's behavior that morning.

- As Bobby returns from therapy, it might be prudent to let his nurse know that he worked particularly hard at walking and may require a nap before he can eat his lunch safely.

What these examples demonstrate is the fact that no group can function in isolation and that information about the child ought not wait for a weekly meeting.

It is also in the best interests of the child and family to tear down any fences or boundaries that a specialty group may have erected around their own "territory." It is important to focus energy on integrated efforts.

*It is not unusual in our program for the physician to pop in and interact with the child during a speech and language session. The psychologist might participate in "speech group." The speech pathologist does stimulation therapy while the physical therapist is positioning the child on the mat.*

# The King's People

Having argued that professionals must be willing to cross into others' fields of expertise in interacting with the child and the family, the remainder of the chapter is organized to define the individual roles on the team.

## Medical Staff

The medical portion of the team is generally considered to include the physiatrist, the pediatric neurologist, the pediatrician, and the nurse—not necessarily in that order.

### Rehabilitation Nurse

Frequently the least acclaimed but often the absolute key to comprehensive care of the traumatically brain-injured child is the nurse. Nurses carry a legacy of stereotyping. Some picture them as "Miss Priss," taking orders from doctors; some view them as Nurse Cratchit, dispensing medication with a leer. Fortunately, most see them as people who work diligently with children and families under any and all circumstances.

In survey after survey, families have described the important role nursing has played in their child's recovery and expressed their appreciation for the support nurses have provided during their times of need.

Nursing goals for the functionally comatose child are medical management, nutritional management, bowel and bladder management, skin integrity, cognitive assessment and stimulation, family support and discharge planning, and family education. Many of the children are admitted with tracheostomies and nasogastric tubes for nutrition. Nurses play a major role in weaning the children from all these "tubes."

**Tracheostomies.** After consultation with the otolaryngologists (more commonly labeled *ear, nose, and throat (ENT) physicians*), the weaning process is begun. Generally, the size of the trach tube is decreased as tolerated to 1, 0, or 00. Then the trach is plugged for brief periods under the watchful eye of nursing staff to ensure that there is adequate air exchange. The length of time the trach is plugged is increased until a 24-hour period has passed.

The ENT doctors then evaluate the appropriateness of removing the cannula (the plastic tube at the trach site). An apnea monitor is used during the weaning process, as well as following decannulation, to ensure appropriate oxygen exchange.

**Feeding tubes.** Many children have a nasogastric (NG) tube or gastrostomy tube in place for feeding. *Nasogastric,* as the name implies, refers to a tube from the nose to the stomach, while a gastrostomy is a tube surgically inserted into the stomach.

*Over the years, we have learned to make this gastrostomy decision earlier. It is much easier to try oral feeding without an NG tube in place, and it is helpful to have the gastrostomy to support nutrition and fluid intake in the recovering child. This decision-making process is discussed further in Chapter 10, Feeding: The Inside Story.*

An easily tolerated formula is used. From continuous feeding, the child is moved gradually to four or five feedings per day. This requires a bolus feeding where the child is able to tolerate one-fourth of the caloric intake without discomfort or vomiting. The goal, ultimately, is a gravity feeding that can be accomplished over a five- to ten-minute period. This allows plenty of time between feedings and fits better into a family schedule.

If a child is admitted with a nasogastric tube and over a few weeks shows limited or no signs of progressing to oral feeding, a gastrostomy tube is considered.

**Bowel and bladder management.** Bowel and bladder management is another team event. The nurses work closely with the physicians and nutritionists to provide the child with the most naturalized approach to management. Catheters should rarely be used because of the risk of infection. Diapers or adult absorbancy products are preferable.

The goal is to help the child move toward bladder training as quickly as possible. This is frequently introduced through routine placement on the commode or, if possible, trips to the bathroom. Parents and therapists act as interpreters in areas outside of the nursing station. Often, the first signs of the child's recognition of physiological need is restlessness or crying. Soon the whole team recognizes the urgency, and a child's means of indicating the wish to go to the bathroom is communicated to the team, whether that is a sign, whining, or use of words.

Bowel management is first tackled through diet, with medications and suppositories as the last resort. Even if a child is sustained by gastrostomy, fiber can be introduced with commercial products designed to help with regularity.

**Family education.** In a sense, all team members function as educators, but the bulk of the responsibility seems to fall on the nurse. This is particularly crucial when children who are functionally comatose are going home on weekend passes. Teaching parents is a very individual matter. Some family members want to know everything right away, and some are very reluctant and must be coaxed to learn to care for their child.

The training begins as parents are encouraged to watch while the child is cared for in the hospital. Then parents gradually assist with the care and become progressively more independent. Two of the most difficult teaching areas are gastrostomy and trach cares.

An extremely helpful bridge in this process is a doll invented by a nurse involved in rehabilitation care of children with brain injuries. The doll has a place to insert an NG tube, a gastrostomy, and a tracheostomy. Families can even use the doll to learn to put on orthoses.

A tracheostomy home-care book written by the nursing staff is helpful in educating families. Additionally, a pediatric brain injury manual authored by the staff is useful in helping families learn to cope with the injury.

All families should be taught CPR.

It is also wise to include a nurse case manager, whose role is to coordinate services with all team members, coordinate discharge to outside agencies, and generally make sure that all play changes at the line of scrimmage are communicated to all team members. Discharge of the child who has needs for medical equipment in the home or residence involves numbers of people and agencies. The nurse case manager oversees the transition to ensure that it goes as smoothly as possible.

### Physicians

The brain injury team usually includes a physiatrist and a pediatric neurologist. A pediatrician also routinely participates in team staffings and is available for the routine medical needs of the child—nutrition, infection, and so on.

The pediatric neurologist takes responsibility for evaluation and treatment of seizures and dysautonomia and for following the patient's neurological and cognitive recovery. This includes the ordering and interpretation of CAT scans, MRI, and all the "alphabet soup" discussed in Chapter 1 on the brain.

Physiatry encompasses the area of physical medicine and rehabilitation. The physiatrist is concerned with the physical management and rehabilitative needs of the child and serves as one of the primary family educators.

In terms of physical management, this doctor works very closely with physical therapy, occupational therapy, and the habilitation technology lab to manage muscle tone through appropriate positioning, serial casting, orthotics, and medication.

The physiatrist also is part of the feeding team, monitoring the timing of videofluoroscopy studies, appropriateness of gastrostomy feedings, and so on.

All physicians contribute to all interventions and pragmatic issues such as readiness for passes, advocating for intense therapies in the community, obtaining preauthorization from providers, conducting research, and advocacy for the needs of the child with brain injury by serving on a multitude of committees and task forces.

## Therapy Staff

"Therapy staff" refers to professionals in physical therapy, occupational therapy, and speech and language pathology. Other parts of the team certainly administer "therapy." For the sake of organization, however, these three areas will be presented as one part of the team, and other "therapies" will be described as part of the child life department.

*In our facility, the physical therapy and occupational therapy areas are our nearest neighbors. That affords us the opportunity to work together and to observe the children in other therapies. In an integrated department such as ours, the traffic flow is conducive to touching bases briefly with other therapists and keeping abreast of the child's changes, moods, etc.*

## Physical Therapy, Occupational Therapy, and Speech-Language Pathology at Levels 4 and 3

At Levels 4 and 3, physical therapy and occupational therapy overlap in providing range of motion exercises to prevent contractures, positioning in bed, and preliminary adaptations to the child's main means of mobility. Wheelchairs and strollers are continually modified to accommodate the changes in the child's muscle control.

A useful development in providing for the mobility needs of children with brain injuries is a wheelchair which allows flexibility in the assessment process as positioning decisions are being made. It is comprised of upholstered cushions and hook-and-loop fasteners. Temporary inserts are used until more permanent decisions can be made regarding seating orthoses.

A host of temporary lap trays is used to provide support to the shoulders as well as a work surface for the child. If the child requires a permanent lap tray, custom trays can be designed and built. Issues such as positioning, mobility, and communication are addressed by the team prior to construction of the lap tray.

The need for casting and orthoses is continually monitored. The physiatrist and therapists begin to design splints and casts to reduce tone and contractures.

In the case of an agitated patient, a sidelyer is used to position and allow the child respite from the uncontrolled movement.

If the patient exhibits sufficient range of motion, ankle stability, and head control, prone standers are used in therapy and ultimately are transferred to the ward for evening use. A prone stander consists of a table with supporting devices and straps that allows the child to stand safely and bear weight.

It is also at Levels 4 and 3 that occupational therapy and speech-language professionals work together with nurses to provide oral stimulation. Once a videofluoroscopy has been done to rule out aspiration, the occupational therapist and the speech-language pathologist will initiate a feeding program, working closely with the nurses to increase the quantity of food and extend the range of textures the child is able to tolerate.

The occupational therapist and the speech-language pathologist assess the child's responses to auditory, tactile, olfactory, and visual stimulation. As motor control improves, the child is channeled through purposeful movement on the therapy mat. (An in-depth discussion of therapy activities is provided in Chapter 7, The Functionally Comatose Child.)

For those children discharged at Levels 4 and 3, the final decisions regarding wheelchair inserts, adaptive equipment, car seats, and equipment for the home are finalized.

The occupational therapist and the physical therapist also complete a photo series that instructs the family with range-of-motion exercises and adapted sitting positions to be used in the home. Orthoses and splints are also illustrated. These photos, taken with an instant camera, personalize the manual and are much more efficient than line drawings.

### Physical Therapy, Occupational Therapy, and Speech-Language Pathology at Levels 2 and 1

As the child progresses cognitively and motorically, the physical therapist begins to focus more on independent ambulation or appropriate assistive devices. Pool therapy becomes an important aspect of treatment, affording the child the opportunity of improved balance in the water. As progress is made, the child is moved to shallower water, which places increased demands on balance and strength.

Wheelchair mobility is also evaluated with assistive devices such as a one-arm-drive wheelchair. The physical therapist works closely with a powered mobility team that includes an occupational therapist and a rehabilitation engineer. They assess the child's abilities and needs for a powered wheel chair. As with electronic communication devices, powered mobility evaluations frequently are postponed until much later in the child's recovery.

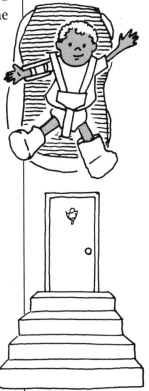

As discharge approaches, the physical therapist works with the family in car transfers and safe motor vehicle transportation. It is critical that car seats and restraints be adapted to meet the transportation needs of the child. Therapists help the family make decisions regarding adaptation of the home to safely meet the physical needs of the child. For example, can the family bring a wheelchair into the home? Can they get the chair into the bathroom, or do they need a commode? How will the child bathe and shower?

The physical therapist, the occupational therapist, and the therapeutic recreation specialist help the child and family explore the child's potential to resume some physical activities. Along with the physician, they provide a list of Dos and Don'ts.

Level 2 is defined by a child's ability to follow commands or gestured requests. It is at this point that the speech-language pathologist can begin to assess the child's overall communication skills and, with the psychologist, provide input as to the child's level of understanding and optimum means of eliciting communication.

If augmentative communication has been initiated, the speech-language pathologist will work with the family, the occupational therapist, and the nurses to choose photos, line drawings, and other aids to design a communication system.

As the child becomes increasingly oriented, the focus shifts more toward utilization of cognitive and language skills to maximize independent functioning in all activities of daily living.

To accomplish this, there must be a great deal of coordination and communication among all team members. For example, at Levels 2 and 1, occupational therapy focuses on functional daily activities such as self-feeding, hygiene, dressing, and age-appropriate kitchen activities. Deficit areas such as visual field cuts, reduced strength and coordination, and impaired judgment are assessed with recommendations provided to parents and other team members to accommodate the child's needs.

Cross-disciplinary teams such as speech-language pathology and occupational therapy will collaborate on cognitive activities that enhance the child's ability to function independently.

- For example, Becca reads a recipe in occupational therapy, carries out the sequenced steps to bake brownies, then brings them to the speech and language group to pass them out and practice conversational skills.

- Timothy and his occupational therapist might work on finding friends' names in the phone book. Having generated a list, he might then place some calls during language therapy.

- Damon may choose to write a book on the computer during speech and language, then illustrate it in occupational therapy.

Outings away from the hospital are excellent opportunities to integrate activities across disciplines. For example, the therapeutic recreation specialist may work with the physical therapist to assist in navigation and planning use of public transportation. The occupational therapist might focus on money management, while the speech-language pathologist practices basic social communication and survival skills.

Prior to discharge, the occupational therapist administers a formal series of tests to evaluate the child's visual motor functioning, visual motor integration, visual perception, upper extremity strength, and coordination.

The occupational therapist teaches the child and family how to do self-ranging exercises. Adaptive equipment for self-feeding, dressing, and bathing is prescribed.

The speech-language pathologist performs a series of tests to determine receptive and expressive vocabulary levels, auditory comprehension, and processing skills, as well as verbal reasoning and expressive language skills. Articulation is assessed, if appropriate, with recommendations for augmentative communication if necessary. Decisions regarding the use of augmentative communication with children who have traumatic brain injuries are more thoroughly discussed in Chapters 8 and 9, which describe the child at Levels 2 and 1.

As with other therapies, the speech-language pathologist, the physical therapist, and the occupational therapist work with school and community agencies to coordinate appropriate services following discharge. More specific information regarding transitioning to school is provided in Chapter 11.

# Family Services

The professionals involved in providing family services include the social worker, the psychologist, the child life specialist, and the therapeutic recreation specialist.

## Social Services

When a family is admitted to a rehabilitation setting, the child may need to be transferred from the acute care setting. Families have already bonded with the staff in those settings, and the transition may be difficult.

It is important to communicate with the family prior to their admission and offer an opportunity to meet with the staff and tour the facility.

This communication can be carried out in several ways, but it is extremely useful for the physician, the social worker, the intake coordinator, and the case manager to meet with the parents and, if appropriate, with the child prior to admission.

As the family prepares for the move, the social worker gathers information that enables the team to know the patient better—information such as brothers' and sisters' names and ages, names of close friends and pets, schools the child has attended, food preferences, and so on. This is basic information, but as the staff begin to orient the child, it is invaluable.

BIO INFO
NAME _John_
BROTHERS _3_
SISTERS _1_
PETS _Bronc the Snake_

The social worker also acts as an advocate for the family, providing the team with feedback as to how the family is dealing with the hospitalization, their external stresses, and any complaints or compliments they may have.

Once the child is ready for weekend passes, the social worker provides the team with an update as to how the family responded to the pass and any particular pitfalls that were encountered.

The financial impact on the family can be a tremendous strain, and family services assist by providing families with the names of appropriate county agencies. With this information in hand, the family can begin the long and laborious process of obtaining waivered charges for services for those children who will continue to need intensive medical and therapeutic services once they return home.

This may mean that the family will have to move to a more accessible house or apartment. Sometimes this is *the* major stumbling block to discharge. It is important, therefore, to explore options early in the hospitalization if there are obvious physical barriers to the child returning to the present home.

Certainly, one of the most important services the social worker and psychology staff offer is in helping the family deal with the grieving process. Many families are still in a state of shock and sometimes denial during the acute stages of the child's rehabilitation. Time and again, the

*We have learned through experience to begin the discharge process on admission. The social worker institutes this by helping the family explore community resources that will be available to assist with their child's return home or, when necessary, seeking long-term rehabilitative care in an appropriate facility.*

*One of our most effective retreats was one in which we hired a comedienne to help heal our wounds with laughter. More about that in Chapter 14, Taking Care of You (While You're Taking Care of Others).*

team needs reminders that the family is not ready to move beyond that initial level of their grief.

As time passes, it is natural and important that families move through various levels of anger, resentment, anxiety, depression, and sometimes guilt. These are expected responses but are still difficult for the family and staff.

Family services can help all those involved with the child through this time by providing not only support for the family but for the staff as well. It is during this time staff is given permission to verbalize their fears, disappointments, and frustrations. It is an important time to share laughter as a team.

### Psychology

As described in the preceding paragraphs, psychology and social work often provide the supportive network for family and staff. During the initial period of recovery, the psychologist may spend more time with parents, siblings, and friends than with patients themselves. One important activity is to provide families and friends with concrete suggestions as to how to visit a child who is in a functional coma, confused, or agitated. The psychologist meets with peers prior to their visit and discusses what to expect and how to respond.

The psychologist most generally becomes involved with the child at Level 2, when the child comprehends and begins to respond to language.

*Sometimes when we just mention behavior in rounds, the child magically changes. We have no idea whether this is due to the wonderful skills of the psychologist—or to the team's increased self-examination as to how we might individually be contributing to the child's negative behaviors, which produces a conscious adjustment of our behavior!*

The psychologist gathers information from parents and the school regarding the emotional and academic development of the child prior to the accident. There is so much insight to be gained by knowing how the child performed in school and at home *before* the injury.

### Behavior Management

As behavioral issues arise—and they almost always do—the psychologist helps to establish a consistent team approach. The psychologist and the speech-language pathologist advocate for the child by reminding everyone where the child is cognitively functioning. The behavior management approach has to be established at a level that makes sense to a child. It is of no use to rationalize with a child who lacks the language comprehension or reasoning skills to respond to your words.

The psychologist provides concrete suggestions to help staff encourage initiation, facilitate participation, or decrease outbursts. This may involve stickers, charts, and rewards. All reinforcers must be immediate and tangible, because most of the children do not yet have the skills to understand delayed rewards.

Other obvious areas of management might include increased rest periods for the child, reduced noise and distraction, or frequent changes in activity.

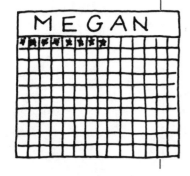

### Cognitive Therapy

At Level 2, the psychologist also interacts directly with the child, focusing on the cognitive needs. Activities are described in Chapters 8 and 9 on Levels 2 and 1.

### Bridging to the School

At Level 1, there is an increased emphasis on school involvement as discharge becomes imminent. The psychologist takes responsibility for inviting appropriate school personnel to attend conferences and observe the child in therapy.

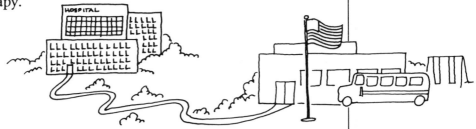

Returning to school can be frightening to the injured child and the family. There may also be some apprehension on the part of the teacher and classmates. An effective means of reducing these anticipatory jitters is to videotape a message from the hospitalized child to the classmates. The psychologist then uses this videotape to describe to the students how hard Paul has been working, suggest things they can do to help Paul when he returns, and answer any questions they might have.

### Personality Changes

There is also an increased focus on the child's social awareness, social appropriateness, and social-interaction effectiveness. The psychologist is active not only in working with the child, but also assisting families in dealing with a child who presents not merely cognitive changes but alterations in personality as well.

### Discharge Testing

As discharge approaches, the psychologist administers a psychoeducational test battery to evaluate the need for special education programming, identify the nature of residual deficits, and determine education intervention strategies.

This battery may include the Wechsler Intelligence Scale for Children—Revised, the Woodcock-Johnson Psycho-Educational Battery, the French Pictorial, and Leiter International for nonverbal children.

There is also an assessment as to the need for future psychological counseling and behavior programming. The psychologist provides outpatient counseling or, when more appropriate, assists the family in finding community resources. Further considerations for discharge are addressed in Chapter 11, on discharge.

### Teacher

In many facilities, a teacher is assigned to the hospital by the public school district. If the child is hospitalized for more than two weeks, the teacher can be involved on a daily basis. The materials are obtained from the child's school district whenever possible. The teacher becomes involved with the child at Level 2 and follows the child until discharge.

In some rehabilitation programs, children attend classrooms for students with traumatic brain injuries. This option affords the opportunity to transition the child more gradually to the mainstream classroom. This will be described more fully in Chapter 11 on discharge.

### Child Life Specialist

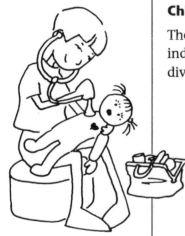

The child life specialist fills a very important role as child advocate. This individual provides opportunities for medical play, socialization, and diversion.

**Medical play.** Using dolls and medical equipment toys, the child life specialist prepares the child for procedures such as IV insertion, casting, staple removal, and so forth. During play with the child, the child life specialist is a careful observer of the child's reaction and adjustment to the hospital stay.

Medical play gives children an opportunity to discuss what will happen and, when possible, gives them some power to choose when and how the procedure will take place.

If possible, it is a good idea to designate a dedicated "procedure room" in which to carry out many of the routine procedures. This accomplishes several things:

- Children are not subjected to procedures in their room or play area.

- The room can be furnished with items to divert the child's attention during the procedure.

- The children are allowed to choose the decorations prior to the procedure, giving them a sense of control over the procedure.

The child life specialist accompanies the child to the procedure, providing diversion and comfort.

**Socialization.** The child life staff, along with the therapeutic recreation specialist, represent one of the most ambitious, creative groups of people in the hospital. They manage to provide activities not only to meet the needs of the vastly different types of patients, but to provide outlets for the families.

In addition to their daily activities, they manage to bring in puppies, clowns, sports heroes, and an occasional singer or two. They arrange for crazy hat days, Hawaiian days, carnival days, bingo nights, teen nights, etc. They take numbers of children out to local pizza places, the ball game, ice shows, and whatever else is in town.

They, like the rest of the team, focus on the cognitive and physical progress of the child. Their observations of the child's use of leisure time, safety and judgment out in the community, and ability to relate to others on the ward are very helpful information to determine the child's readiness for discharge.

### Therapeutic Recreation Specialist

This staff member works very closely with the child life staff but also adds a separate dimension to the team. The therapeutic recreation specialist is trained to evaluate the leisure interests of the child and help the child learn to cope and adjust to physical and cognitive changes after the accident.

It is the therapeutic recreation specialist who can often be seen accompanying a child for the first semi-independent trip on the elevator to the gift shop, or the cafeteria, or on a supervised walk around the hospital.

This team utilizes activities to increase strength and endurance, improve fine motor skills, and increase memory, attention, and psychosocial skills. Most afternoons there is a procession of little bodies, big bodies, and wheelchairs that head down to the swimming pool to let off steam and perform in water what their bodies can no longer do on dry land.

Throughout the hospital stay and during discharge, therapeutic recreation staff work with the child and family to explore ways to resume or adapt leisure and recreational activities—certainly a critical component to the child's emotional and physical well-being.

● ● ● ● ●

This has been a discussion of how our "team" functions. Roles, responsibilities, and even the professionals who comprise the team vary from center to center. *Who* is not so important as *how* the team functions.

Each team will have its strengths and weaknesses. It is made up of human beings with human characteristics. *Communication is critical.* But even with communication, there are disagreements.

- Discussion flows back and forth regarding the effects of a particular medication—"relaxing" (good for the child's muscles) but "sedating" (bad for attention).

- Parties may disagree as to when to do a videofluoroscopy—"has been handling own secretions" versus "too agitated for an accurate study."

Disagreement is not unhealthy. It promotes discussion and problem solving. Red cheeks are stimulating. But disagreement should not include argument about who does what. For example, everyone is a cognitive retrainer, all observe eye tracking, everyone is concerned with oral stimulation.

Roles must overlap. To do that, boundaries shift to meet the needs of the child and family. It is they who are the center of the team.

# The Family

Let us begin this chapter with a reminder that neither of us is a family therapist. This chapter will not teach counseling techniques for families.

This chapter will discuss the accident's impact on the family, suggest ways to help families supportively, provide suggestions *from* families on how best to help, and suggest adaptations when the family's language and culture are different from your own. Included are case studies of families who have taught us lessons of patience, acceptance, and laughter. The special case of brothers, sisters, and friends will be discussed.

We have worked with hundreds of families (usually shoulder to shoulder in therapy and at bedside), sat in many family conferences, followed children and families for many years after discharge in an outpatient clinic, and worked with families in local, state, and national advocacy groups. We are presenting our experience, and we hope you find it helpful.

● ● ● ● ●

## Guiding Principles in Working with Families

Two important points about working with families must be underscored at the outset of this chapter. The first is that there are excellent resources available that are extremely helpful for families undergoing the trauma that results when their child sustains a brain injury.

*We are both parents and our children have been sick. In fact, one of Candace's children had meningitis as an infant and now has a hearing loss in one ear. But we have never had a child who had a brain injury in a terrible accident. That tragedy is unfathomable to us, that grief unimaginable.*

It is important to have these types of excellent resources available for families. Many family members and professionals have contributed thoughtful and helpful information in these booklets. Additionally, you will learn a great deal from the family's perspective.

The second important point to remember is that, unless you have a child with a traumatic brain injury, **never ever** assume that you know what the family is experiencing, because you don't. It is completely discrediting to the family to say, "I know how you must feel."

# The Family Is Hurt

The best way to visualize the impact of a child's injury on a family is to imagine that the whole family is riding the bike that is hit by the car; or that the entire family falls off the back of a pick-up truck or falls into a lake and nearly drowns. Everyone gets hurt—mom, dad, brothers, sisters, and grandparents. And when one includes other relatives and friends to this group, the injury list become very long indeed.

It is crucial to recognize this long list of people as hurt because it is the therapist's responsibility to be helpful and supportive educationally to all people involved.

This is not easy, but it is what pediatric rehabilitation is. It must be family-centered to work. On a very practical level, this means that the family is in therapy, and should be! Much of the time, at least one parent is in therapy, and very often grandmas, grandpas, brothers, and sisters are there too.

This can be tiring, even overwhelming, because it is hard to always be watched by people so invested in their child's progress. But it is so crucial to the child's recovery and family education, that it simply has to be done! Some suggestions on how to make this work are described below.

- Explain what you are doing, and why.

- Don't be afraid to change activities if something isn't working.

- Ask the family for advice about the best ways to reach their child in therapy.

- Have fun! Therapy need not be so terribly serious as to ignore the child's emotional recovery. It is important to laugh with the child and the family when something funny happens or is said.

- Keep a box of tissues handy. Family members often cry in therapy—usually because their child is doing something new—and it should not be surprising for you to see those tears.

# The Family as Customer

Families seem to view therapy in a reverent manner—they expect the best therapists, the full treatment session time, the best equipment—and they should. They are your customers!—no kidding! They are your employer, and it is their satisfaction that is crucial to the success of your organization.

*I personally wish families really saw me for what I am—simply a guide for their child through the maze of recovery. I channel, modify, and encourage responses in a caring, intense, professional manner, but I cannot make children come out of coma, or talk, or remember, or think. I wish I could. There have been children who talked whom I didn't expect to and, of course, children who didn't regain speech whom I expected would.*

*What I can give the family is my very best shot each session, combining my education, experience, and hope that their child will be guided toward progress. And if progress doesn't happen, I can be as sad and disappointed as I feel. Conversely, it requires humility and maturity to place the accolades of a successful recovery where they belong—not on my shoulders but on the smaller shoulders of the child surrounded by family members.*

*It is, after all, the result of the child's work that gets everyone to where they want to be. In fact, I wish our pediatric rehabilitation department had huge yellow caution signs at the entrance that said: Caution! Children at Work. Therapy is work for the child. It is work for me too, but I'm getting paid.*

# Where Have All the Families Gone?

Society is changing the word *family*. It is becoming more and more unusual in pediatric rehabilitation to meet with a mother, a father, sisters, and brothers who have a station wagon in the parking ramp and a dog and cat at home. Families are often single parents, divorced parents unexpectedly brought together by the sudden tragedy, blended families with a variety of stepsisters and stepbrothers, and parents split apart by the distance of the rehabilitation center from their home. And, sadly, there are times when the child's parents visit very rarely.

The team social worker provides information to the team about the constellation of the family. You must know who is who and, most importantly, who is legally responsible for the child. It is crucial to treat family members respectfully, regardless of your personal opinions.

# Cultural Diversity

Practitioners today will work with many families for whom a language other than English is the language spoken at home, and whose culture is different from the prevailing American traditions. Solicit the aid of any of your fellow workers who have greater fluency in second languages and who are familiar with the other cultures reflected in your area.

The suggestions that follow may be of some assistance in situations where you are not conversant in the family's language.

- Have formally trained language interpreters to call upon. This includes sign language interpreters for parents or other family members with hearing impairments.

- Learn how to work with an interpreter. Many interpreter programs for people with hearing impairments offer free courses on how to use an interpreter effectively. There are important courtesies to observe, the most crucial of these being to state briefly what you want to say, *wait* for the interpreter to say it, and *wait* for the family to respond.

It is especially important when working with a child who has English as a second language to explain to the interpreter that you need the child's *exact* verbal responses translated. Some interpreters may have a tendency to phrase the child's verbal responses in more adult language using complete sentences—a nice gesture but one which fails to provide the clinical information needed to work effectively with the child.

- Ask the family about their culture. What holidays do they celebrate? What language is spoken in the home? Do they have special ways they would like their child handled? touched? spoken to? Could they teach you about their culture? What characteristics are most important?

- Have written treatment goals translated into the language of the family.

It is most important to recognize the differences in culture, respect these differences, and learn from them. Common experience shows that parents are very willing teachers of culture and vocabulary. One need only ask.

# The Whole Gang: Brothers, Sisters, Grandparents, and Friends

Brothers and sisters of the hurt child are a very special case. They are understandably pushed to the "back burner" while parental energy, love, and concern surround the hospitalized child. Often they have new people caring for them, and different food is dropped off by family friends.

*Most of us know a little of a lot of languages but are frustrated by lack of fluency in a second or third language. For example, my Spanish is at a two-year level and my Norwegian at 14 months. I know a few Chinese, Russian, and Rumanian words. I know finger spelling, but my signing is at a toddler level.*

*Nowhere am I more struck by my communication ineffectiveness than when I meet a family and child with English as a second language. After all, at the core of speech and language pathology is effective verbal communication, even though a great deal of communication can be conveyed with gesture and facial effect.*

Their schedule is greatly interrupted. They visit in the hospital, but it seems there, too, their hurt sibling gets all the toys, the computer programs, the swimming pool, and special presents from everyone. This feeling of being ignored can turn into many behaviors—acting out, quiet and withdrawn behavior, and guilt about the angry and jealous feelings.

Thankfully there are professionals whose job it is to help brothers and sisters understand and cope. These people include psychologists, social workers, and child life specialists.

The best thing rehabilitation clinicians can do for siblings is *pay attention to them!* When they visit therapy, ask about their life, explain who you are and what you are doing, and give them a chance to play with the toys, use the computer, ride the adapted tricycle. These children are hurt too, and any touch, smile, present, or turn you can allow them makes them feel a little more special.

Grandparents are often present as well, and occasionally they have a mistrust or suspicion of the medical model. Again, it is important to welcome them to therapy and explain what you are doing. They can become excellent, supportive advocates and add affection and laughter to a therapy session.

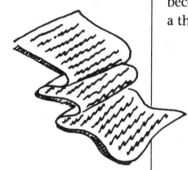

As mentioned previously, friends can be on the injury list too. The age of the child influences the role of friends. When a child is young (as in preschool, kindergarten, or early elementary grades), the friends often visit at the child's home during weekend passes. Occasionally, they visit the child in the hospital. When that is the case, it is helpful to tell them what their friend is learning to do and how they can be helpful.

As children become older (later elementary grades, junior high, and senior high), the friends are visiting frequently—sometimes in droves! Ask the family's permission, and give team educational sessions to groups of older friends. It is important for them to understand brain injury, what their friend is learning to do, and what constitutes helpful friendship.

Friends should be given specific suggestions for ways to be supportive. Give ideas about appropriate gifts and activities to do when visiting. Reading to their friend from the school or community newspaper, showing pictures, describing activities they and their friend have done together, and playing cognitively appropriate games are all useful.

It is also very important for you to appreciate and respect the recovering child's privacy. There may be times when the child is nonresponsive, incredibly fatigued, agitated and crying because of discomfort, or behaviorally inappropriate. Under these circumstances, it would be more respectful to the child and the family to request that friends not visit therapy. The family/therapy team may need to become more restrictive about visitation.

# Communication with Families

You have a family in your care who has been thrown into the morass of medicine. They don't know the terminology, who you are, or what in the world is going on. How and what you communicate is very crucial to the family's education. The following points should help.

- Tell them who you are and what you do.

  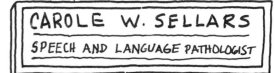

  My name is Carole Sellars. I am a speech-language pathologist. My training is to help Sara pay more attention to her environment and evaluate her ability to eat safely. I will be seeing Sara twice a day, and you are always welcome in my therapy classes.

  or

  I am a speech-language pathologist. My job on the treatment team is to help Sara become less confused and remember. I will also be helping her speech get better. I will be seeing her twice a day, and you are always welcome in my therapy sessions.

- Always give caring, honest input. It is never appropriate to argue with parents about what a child is able to do. The child is probably doing more for the parents than you anyway, and the parents are usually right.

- Communicate formally at family-team conferences. It is helpful for staff to meet with families every two to three weeks to discuss therapy progress and goals. Families are given an opportunity to have input into the goals they would like their child to accomplish.

The objective at the first conference is to report on initial evaluation results, and the team shares with the family the specific, measurable goals they expect the child to accomplish by the next conference.

Depending on many factors (such as injury severity, progress, and readiness of the community), the family may have numerous conferences. The final meeting plans for the child's discharge, and discharge goals are presented.

---

### Sample Goals for the Various Stages of Therapy

**Therapy Goals for a Child in Coma**

- A sidelyer will be constructed and adjusted to fit John.
- John will be able to follow brightly colored toys and pictures with his eyes.
- John will have a videofluoroscopy evaluation to determine his ability to eat pureed food safely.
- John's hand splints will be monitored to assure they fit well with no pressure points.

### Therapy Goals for a Child out of Coma

- Kala will rise independently from the floor.

- Kala will safely and independently negotiate a full flight of stairs with railing.

- Kala will be able to provide correct information about her accident and remember the names of three team members.

- Kala will maintain her attention and cooperation for 20 minutes using a sticker reward system.

- Kala will orally eat and drink enough food and liquid to support her nutritional needs.

### Discharge Goals for a Child in Coma

- The sitting support orthosis will be completed and be comfortable. The wheelchair will be ordered and, if not delivered by discharge, a reclining wheelchair will be rented and temporarily modified.

- A picture home program of positioning and range-of-motion activities will be completed for parents and community caregivers.

- An appropriate home-bound infant stimulation program will be found in the local community.

- Parents will take Jeremy out for three day passes and one overnight before discharge.

- Jeremy will tolerate tube feedings without problems, and weight will be monitored to prevent excessive gain.

- All therapy home programs, videos, and written reports will be completed for the family by the day of discharge.

### Discharge Goals for a Child out of Coma

- Susan will complete baseline cognitive, achievement, speech-language, and visual perception testing.

- Susan will be fully independent in dressing with verbal cues.

- Bathroom equipment needs will be assessed.

- Parents will visit the early education program in the community school.

- School educational and therapy staff will attend a planning conference and observe therapies.

- Child life staff will provide specific activities to help Susan transition from hospital to school.

---

These are examples of goals, and the list is not intended to be inclusive. The most helpful thing about having specific goals available for parents from the first conference to the last is that it gives the family the opportunity to focus on the child's current status and what are the next measures of progress. Because recovery from traumatic brain injury is unpredictable, focusing on these increments seems to help families cope.

- Remember that the family is exhausted. Don't expect them to remember what you said. A good rule of thumb is, *Always remember you are talking to people who have been up all night.*

- Help them have the role as historian, supporter, advocate, cheerleader, and planner. Frequently the social worker's first contact with a family is to fill out a profile of the child on nicknames, pets, family information, school information, personality, favorite activities, and favorite friends. Because this information is shared with the child's other therapists, the family's role as historian is very important to the staff's understanding of the child.

- Families do best when they are given education, ongoing support, and the opportunity for constructive action. The education consists of providing unambiguous communication that takes into account the family's language and culture.

Ongoing support is provided on site or in the local community. Constructive action involves putting the family in contact with such advocacy groups as the National Head Injury Foundation, the state head injury chapter, Mothers Against Drunk Driving, and school advocacy organizations. Assisting the family in contacting Social Security, insurance firms, state and federal financial assistance programs, and attorneys is also concretely helpful.

Many states, including Minnesota, provide medical assistance to children with disabilities who live at home with their families. Only the child's income and property are counted when determining eligibility for medical assistance. This program is commonly known as TEFRA (because it was attached to the Tax Equity and Fiscal Responsibility Act of 1982 when it was passed by Congress). It is very important for families to obtain information on this funding option, and this can be done by contacting the hospital social worker. This program may cover services such as home health care, therapy, personal care services, medical supplies, equipment, and prescribed drugs.

# When a Family Member Has Died in the Accident

Working in a pediatric brain injury program almost guarantees that there will be times when the accident is so tragic that a parent or other family member is killed in the accident. The remaining family members are often afraid to tell the child, or they wonder when is the best time.

Experience has shown that children should be told immediately after they demonstrate the ability to understand some language. A recovering child at this stage does not yet possess insight and thus grief into the loss, but it helps the family immeasurably to let the child know.

Often the recovering child begins to grasp the tragedy only when at Level 1 of consciousness and some memory has returned. It seems that the child begins to grieve at the time of discharge and concretely understands that loss on a day-to-day basis.

Families are encouraged to take pictures of the funeral so the child eventually will have concrete information to help facilitate grieving.

# Will Parents Ever Go Home?

The experience in most facilities is that mothers and sometimes fathers will be right there, every day and every night, until children can talk and accurately report on their hospital day. It is useless and perhaps disrespectful to suggest to mothers that they go home. They don't. They won't. They say they just can't. I wouldn't either.

# Lessons from Parents

This chapter emphasizes again and again (perhaps ad nauseam) what *we can teach* families. We can, of course, teach a great deal about professional concerns. But obviously this relationship between parents and therapists is reciprocal. The following are a few lessons I have been taught by parents.

**Heidi, age 8:** I was taught patience. Heidi was 8 years old when she received a brain injury in a car accident. When discharged from our facility eight months later, she was alert but unresponsive to language.

For five years following her discharge, I saw her in an out-patient clinic. She was still alert, responsive to sensory input, and able to smile. She was also still unresponsive to language.

One July afternoon Heidi and her parents drove the 200 miles for her annual checkup. She was able to follow simple verbal commands and identify pictures on request. I was ecstatic! Six years after injury, she had moved into Level 2 of consciousness. I bubbled with joy to the parents. They smiled at my enthusiasm, but their eyes said, "Didn't you ever think she would? Oh, ye of little patience—we knew she would."

**Michelle, age 16:** I was taught laughter. Michelle received a brain injury in a car accident while a junior in high school. Her parents attended most therapy sessions. When Michelle began talking, her sense of humor was exceeded only by that of her parents.

They laughed with her and, before long, we were all sharing jokes and puns. We had verbal "oneupsmanship" contests in therapy, and I learned quickly that her parents not only expected me to laugh in therapy—they required it because their family life was based on loving repartee, and for a brief period of my life I was honored to be a part of it. Laughing along is a lovely symptom of true acceptance.

**Natasha, age 2:** I was taught acceptance. Tash received a severe anoxic injury in an electrocution injury with cardiac arrest. Her mother stayed with her in the hospital while her father and older sister lived at home 250 miles away. When I first met Tash she was very cognitively impaired and could only blink to loud sound and grimace to light touch. Her eyes were open but it didn't appear that she could see.

Tash was discharged four months later at the same level cognitively. Her mother, however, had grown to accept her daughter's limitations and yet had hope that she would get better. She loved and accepted her daughter with such visible care, it was a touching lesson.

She made elaborate hair ribbons to match every outfit, made an autograph quilt for Tash's crib for all of us to sign, decorated the bedside with very personal and colorful toys and pictures, and bought Tash a fish aquarium for Christmas so "she could watch the fish and learn to see." I am still awed by parental acceptance.

# Advice from Parents

A fitting conclusion to this chapter is *real* advice from parents about how best to help. Each parent was asked to write a letter about how professionals can help families when their child is recovering from a brain injury.

### Michelle's Mother's Point of View

When she was first injured and comatose, it was so hard to believe that she was so seriously hurt—physically she was kind of a Sleeping Beauty and, in spite of the tubes and monitors, it was still easier to believe that she would simply wake up and ask, "What happened to January?"

By the time she went to rehabilitation, I was terrified—she was no longer in a coma, but beginning from square one—she looked so damaged. I had to face my fears, my old biases about people with disabilities, some that I had not ever acknowledged to myself. Where was my old Michelle? and what would my new Michelle be like? The love, acceptance, and encouragement as Michelle re-emerged, and the optimism about her future and her capabilities, gave me hope.

Mixed with empathy and warmth was a professionalism, an assuredness that you knew what you were about (as well as still learning about recovery from brain injury) that was *very* reassuring.

As I look back on those dazed days I wonder that much penetrated my own fears: what if I simply could not handle this, what if I didn't have the right stuff to help her (whatever that was!)? The staff was supportive and respectful of my need to be the kind of mom I am: to let me be there when I needed to be; and to get away when I needed to get away.

It is so painful to watch your child be put through the rigors of rehabilitation—when all you wish is that they could be put in cotton batting and rest their way into healing—emotions range from overwhelming grief to rampant fury. I can scarcely describe the agony of a "thermometer, apple juice, and aspirin" parent who is suddenly faced with "to trach or not to trach?; when to repair the craniotomy," when all the life-saving and life-serving procedures *feel* for all the world like still another assault on your child's body . . . It wears and scrapes down deep inside where mother-bear fierceness lives, and a need to protect has already been violated. Perspective is out of whack; intense longing to do something to *fix* things exists in the same reality as long, slow days of recovery in teeny, tiny steps.

The most helpful was the team's groundedness and calmness in the knowledge that recovery was proceeding as expected (as unfamiliar as the territory was for *us*) or their rejoicing over more rapid gains (though they might have seemed minuscule to us who were wanting quick and complete) helped me to get a grasp on realistic expectations; and a handle on what I could *actually* do in the real world to be helpful to Michelle's recovery. The concrete suggestions, recommendations about equipment, adaptations for car travel, adjustments at home, optimism, humor! said that the devastating and earth-shattering were survivable, could be handled, could be managed.

Sometimes you trust because you have to—it's out of your knowledge, it's out of your experience, it's out of your hands. It is a scary business, but it helps if the people you are working with are honest about their limitations and ready to give you what they can. Their own confidence in what they are doing; their ever and ongoing research in the field of brain injury translated to me that Michelle was receiving the best of what was out there.

Staff was always *available* for questions, concerns, and discussion, and extended that to a family/friend meeting—most helpful to them to ask their own questions. The family-centered approach was one of the stronger lures for me—we needed your kind of support, the acknowledgment that the family is *forever* changed.

## Michelle's Father's Point of View

Acceptance does finally come—that yes, my beautiful daughter has been brain-injured and things will be different for her and her family for the rest of our lives.

The first thing that helped me a lot during Michelle's recovery were the family conferences. Here in one room were her doctors, primary nurse, occupational therapist, physical therapist, and speech pathologist . . . and, of course, us, her parents. This was not just a collection of people with various vocations—these were persons with skills and experiences whose purpose was to help my daughter to the best of their abilities. It was obvious they cared about Michelle as they discussed with us and each other what her goals would be and how they would help her to achieve them.

The most helpful thing for me was to be able to witness some of the occupational, physical, and speech therapy sessions. There are a couple of points that stand out in my mind about these sessions. The first is the respect that was always shown to Michelle by each therapist. Sometimes some "prodding" was necessary during a session and this was always done in a respectful way. The second is that I always felt at ease in asking a question of the therapist. My questions were always answered in a polite way, and sometimes the answer was "I don't know" or "We'll have to wait and see"—and that's okay too. The truth is there are a lot more "unknowns" than "knowns" in a brain injury recovery, but my experience has been that the therapists maintain hope right along with the parents. My advice to therapists, then, is to be respectful, cheerful, and hopeful.

## Talking about Jodi's Recovery

As parents of Jodi, our brain-injured daughter, we found ourselves on a roller coaster of emotions and struggles. Up and down between grief and hope, sometimes feeling "in control" of the home front, relationships, and our hurt daughter's care, and more often overwhelmed with undone tasks, unmet needs, and Jodi's struggle for recovery.

I appreciated Jodi's therapists' ability to interact with me through the tears and emotions. They expressed compassion but could still carry on their work. That, after all, was what I wanted more than anything else, to have them help Jodi.

I was always so anxious to hear what Jodi was able to do in therapy, preferring to see it for myself. I so appreciated the therapists' willingness to let me (and/or my parents, husband, daughters, or close friends) sit in therapy sessions. I wanted to be able to complement the therapists' work with Jodi. It helped me a lot to be able to "do something."

The respect we saw for Jodi and ourselves was another important plus in our interaction with Jodi's therapists. Their recognizing, enjoying, and respecting our uniqueness made our relationships comfortable and meaningful. They were honest and real with us and accepted us as we were.

I'm sure it isn't easy to relax the "professional distance," but from our perspective, it only enhanced our trust and appreciation for those working with Jodi. We hope their rewards for their work are great. They gave us so much.

# Philosophy of Therapy

The word *therapy,* according to the Oxford English Dictionary, is from the Greek *to heal.* This is a heavy mantle, taking therapy above the realm of "fixing" or "changing." However, the definition assumes an end result that is finished and, in fact, healed. Yet therapy is a process toward change that often does not result in normalcy or perfection.

It is that process, that therapeutic milieu, that we would like to discuss before embarking on the chapters that present specific therapeutic goals and procedures. We want you to understand clearly the dynamic, fluid nature of therapy that, in the case of children with brain injuries, is often completely dependent on the therapist's being willing to trust intuition, change activities, accept limitations, and veritably "fly by the seat of the pants!"

We have come to believe therapy is many things. We would like to outline a few.

## Therapy Is Intelligent and Carefully Considered

It is important not to underestimate your professional training and academic, theoretical knowledge. That is always the core of your session. You know the fundamentals of neurology, anatomy, language, psychology, and learning theory. Your vocabulary is replete with professional terminology and it is important that you give credit to that expertise.

One way to keep this in mind is to imagine the major professor of your master's committee walking in and asking you to describe the rationale of your therapy. The materials you are using augment that rationale, but the process you and the child are wrapped in is the theoretical construct of your therapy.

Describe that theory to the family and your professional peers so they know it too. It is much too valuable to keep secret. Additionally, families have confidence in you when you share with them what you know.

## Therapy Is Dynamic

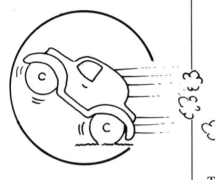

This means that therapy is not static. It moves. It changes. It responds quickly to changes in a child. The child is always your barometer of change. If children look bored, they are. If their eyes are lit, their mind is. If they look confused, they are. If they are disappointed that the session is over, you have done a good job. If your therapy does not lightly skim just above the child's performance capacity, they will have nothing to reach for.

The child is always the mirror of your skill. It is that mirror that reflects your willingness to be fluid, to move with the child.

## Therapy Is Fun

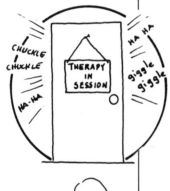

When reciprocal laughter emits from your therapy room, you can be sure healing is happening. This does not mean that laughter happens always, but when it does you are cementing a relationship with a child.

## Therapy Is the Framework for Self-Esteem

It is the mechanism by which you show the child and family what they can do. The stage is carefully set for success and praise. Even with failure to do the task, there is positive feedback: "Matt, you are looking so serious. I know you are trying so hard." For that moment, the child is the best—the best at smiling, the best at listening, the best at trying.

## Therapy Is Exhausting

It takês tremendous energy to observe, encourage, structure, challenge, and laugh—especially when the child is unable to give much in return. Add to that a family that is watchful, expectant, hopeful, desperate . . . and you quickly deplete your energy reserve. What replenishes it is the promise that this child will get better.

# Therapy Is Stimulating

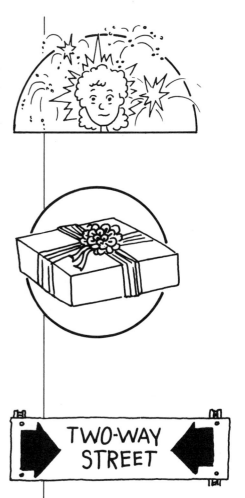

There is a surge of adrenaline that courses through your entire being when a child produces that first sound, follows that first command, remembers a weekend pass. In that one moment, all hours of work are forgotten, and new goals and aspirations are beginning to form. It is the hook that keeps us coming back.

# Therapy Is Reciprocal

Therapy is not only what you do with a child, it is what that child does with you. You touch and are touched in return. You laugh and get a smile in return. This reciprocity of healing is too often overlooked in the venue of a traditional look at the *therapist* doing to the child. It is that small person doing to us big people that keeps us going, keeps us vibrant, keeps us loved, keeps us well.

Children are naturally generous in their gifts. Those daily, unexpected presents swaddle you with trust, love, and laughter. They elicit poignancy, memories, inspiration, and commitment. As you graciously receive these gifts, return them with gifts of your own. Enter this reciprocity of therapy. The healing process is a two-way street.

# 7

# Levels 4 and 3:
# The Functionally Comatose
# Child

This chapter specifically talks about why you probably bought this book—to learn therapy techniques for the child with a traumatic brain injury. It describes the comatose child and the medical hardware and positioning devices, and discusses therapy goals and procedures for the child at Levels 4 and 3. The controversy regarding coma stimulation will also be addressed as a conclusion to this chapter.

## The Child in Coma

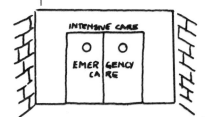

From every viewpoint, a child in a coma is a powerful, overwhelming sight. No college course quite prepares a clinician for the intensive care center and a young child hooked up to all the technological support equipment. This is especially true when the equipment is unfamiliar.

Ask the intensive care nurses to explain the equipment. They are willing to do so. Also, it is very important to understand that the child's medical status has the highest priority at this time in recovery. Always ask the child's nurse if this is a good time to do therapy. If not, come back later or tomorrow.

### In the Tubes!

Bradley was 6 years old when he had a brain injury. Once he could walk and talk, he would point down the hall toward the pediatric intensive care unit and say, "That's where I was **in the tubes!**" Some of the tubes you may encounter are described here.

- Intracranial pressure (ICP) monitor: This is a bolt commonly placed in the space surrounding the child's brain to monitor intracranial pressure. It requires a few stitches when removed, and you may notice children whose hair is shaved in a small area above the forehead, the location of the ICP monitor.

- Tracheostomy: This is an opening made in the child's airway to provide a passage for air exchange and access to suctioning. The tracheostomy may be attached to a ventilator if the child cannot breathe independently.

The nurse suctions mucus from the child's airway by passing a tube down the tracheostomy. A humidity mask is often placed over the opening in the trachea (the stoma) to keep the child's airway moist. Sometime a "nose" is placed on the tracheostomy, so called because it filters air going into the lungs as the nose does.

- Catheters: Frequently the child has a catheter, a tube placed directly in the urethra, to allow for continual collection of urine. It is important to measure urine output accurately, to evaluate functioning of the kidneys and whether they are getting enough oxygen.

- Vital sign monitors: The child commonly has small leads on the chest hooked to machines that monitor oxygen content of the blood, heart rate, and respiratory rate. Sometimes the oxygen content of the blood is measured from a small sample of blood collected from the tip of a finger or toe.

- Feeding tubes: At this point in a child's recovery, the child does not have a gastrostomy (a tube going directly into the stomach for feeding) because it is too early to predict whether or not the child will be able to eat orally. Instead, the child will have either a nasogastric or nasojejunum tube. Both of these tubes go through the child's nose: the nasogastric tube goes to the stomach and the nasojejunum tube goes to the intestines. This nasal tube is taped down with adhesive tape.

Not only are children hooked up to all this equipment, they frequently have very black eyes from the impact of the injury, scars on their faces, and perhaps broken bones or internal injuries which are also being treated. This scenario is explained for those of you who work in a facility with a pediatric intensive care program.

Many of you will never clinically see a child at this stage of recovery, but it is important for you to know that they and their parents have been through this. The comforting news is that the child does not recall the accident or this intensive care stage. Many are interested in touring the intensive care unit once they are recovering, and want to meet the nurses who took such good care of them. Encourage these visits, because they are helpful in orienting the child.

Many professionals in acute rehabilitation, post-acute rehabilitation, and the school systems will first meet Level 4 or 3 children when they are more medically stable. They may still have a tracheostomy, and by this point they often have a feeding tube to the stomach. All other medical paraphernalia generally has been removed. The equipment that prevails now is usually in the physical therapy domain and deserves mention.

## Positioning Equipment

One of the most important considerations for children who are dependent is to position them safely and therapeutically. The philosophy is to provide essential support while encouraging and challenging the child to make active movements.

This is a tightrope for physical therapists to walk, and those who are not in this field must understand and appreciate the challenges. A child without positioning devices can quickly become contracted, deformed, and in pain. Some of the devices that are commonly used to combat these problems are described here.

- Wheelchairs: A wheelchair is not a wheelchair is not a wheelchair. There are many different kinds of wheelchairs including child, youth, adult, light-weight, sport, electric, reclining, one-arm drive, hemi, and ready-made chairs with special support. The choice of appropriate wheelchair is extremely important to the child's recovery and mobility.

- Headrests: Often the headrest needs to be removable to encourage the child to hold the head up a portion of the day and to allow a resting support when the child is tired. Some headrests need a side extension if the child keeps turning the head to one side.

- Sitting Support Orthoses: Some children need only a firm seat and back with a pelvic belt and chest vest to be positioned properly in a wheelchair. Others have much less control or very increased tone and require a molded seat placed in the wheelchair for support. This sitting support orthosis is specially fitted to the child.

- AFO, WHO: The child's feet are often positioned at a 90-degree angle with plastic braces called ankle-foot orthoses (AFO). A wrist-hand orthosis (WHO) is often fabricated by an occupational therapist to promote good hand position.

- Other positioning devices:

  - A sidelyer is often used to help the child position comfortably on the side. Although it looks a little like the "torture rack" from a sixteenth-century French novel, it is used effectively to reduce tone and subsequent agitation and discomfort.

  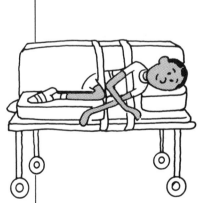

  - A stander is used to help the child position in an upright posture. This allows weight-bearing through the feet which is therapeutic. A prone stander positions the child on the stomach, then the stander is gradually raised upright. A supine stander begins with the child on the back, then the child is positioned upright.

  - There are also special car seats and vests used to safely and therapeutically transport physically dependent children to their homes for passes.

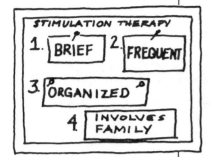

# Stimulation Therapy

This section covers stimulation therapy intervention for the child described as functionally comatose, unable to respond to language. This includes children at Levels 4 and 3. For each level, a behavioral description of the child will be presented, treatment goals outlined, and therapy suggestions offered. Concluding remarks cover the controversy of stimulation therapy.

Terms often used for therapy at this level are *stimulation* or *coma stimulation therapy*. The important features of stimulation therapy include the following principles.

- Therapy should be **brief:** Because the child fatigues quickly and satiates rapidly (gets used to stimulation), stimulation therapy sessions should last no longer than 15 minutes.

- Therapy should be **frequent:** Organized periods of stimulation should be provided eight to ten times a day by clinicians, nurses, and family members.

- Therapy should be **organized:** Make certain that those stimuli that elicit responses are consistently included in the session. It certainly is fine to try other forms of stimuli, but the important focus should be those that consistently elicit a response.

- Therapy should **involve the family.** The family should be given the area around the bedside to decorate with familiar and meaningful items. This ranges from cartoon posters to toys to sports figures to stuffed animals to movie stars to television characters to rock stars. Whatever. Encourage the family to bring in tapes of familiar music and voices of classmates and relatives. It is also helpful to have the family put a guest book at the child's bedside so visitors can sign in and leave notes.

## Level 4: A Generalized Response

The child at Level 4 demonstrates a generalized response to sensory stimuli. In other words, the child arouses to specific stimulation. They most consistently have an **auditory startle** (eye blink to loud sound), response to **visual threat** (eye blink when an object or hand comes rapidly toward their face), and **grimace to light touch** (usually observed by lightly tickling the child's lips with a feather).

The therapeutic goal is simply stated: to elicit responses. Therapy can best be described as doing almost anything that is legal and will elicit a response. The goal is to heighten arousal and awareness.

### Therapy Techniques

Some of the materials that have been helpful in stimulation therapy for children at Level 4 are listed here.

*We store all of our stimulation materials in a plastic file box. This is an easy way to organize the materials and provides a convenient method of carting the materials down the halls of the hospital.*

**Tactile:** fur, feathers, feather duster, soft cloth, brushes, shaving cream, high school cheerleading pompoms, and assorted pieces of fabrics with different textures

**Taste:** food extracts (particularly lemon, raspberry, and strawberry), chocolate syrup, flavored disposable toothbrushes, and lemon glycerine swabs. (These swabs sound wonderfully refreshing but actually taste terrible—be sure to try in your own mouth first what you are putting into the child's!)

**Smell:** chest liniment, flavorings (such as almond, vanilla, and anise), boot and shoe polish, *cheap* perfumes and colognes, and assorted spices (such as chili powder, pizza flavorings, mustard, vinegar, and catsup)

**Visual:** brightly colored toys, fluorescent sponge balls, small flashlight, mirror, birthday party blowers, pinwheels, and kaleidoscopes

**Sound:** loud bike horn, variety of bells at different pitches and intensities, recorded environmental sounds, toys that make animal sounds, wood blocks to bang together, drum, tambourine, and assorted musical tapes

### Therapy Guidelines

The guidelines below are important points to consider at this and every stage of a child's recovery.

- It is important to use your imagination about what may elicit a response in a child. Anything legal and safe will qualify! Be sure to check with the family about possible allergies to smell or taste.

  When you are filling your stimulation kit, think of those things that would arouse you or your child from a deep sleep. That principle should help you understand why a loud bike horn, a feather, a flashlight, liniment, and lemon extract are important to anyone's kit. It also helps explain why photographs of the family, picture books, and music boxes are nice but will not elicit a visible response.

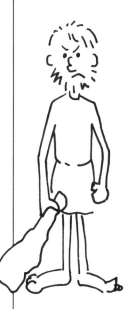

- Because the goal is to elicit responses, you can sometimes feel a little like "Attila the Hun," presenting noises that are loud and smells that are "icky." Explain to parents why you have chosen the materials you have. If a child has a consistent auditory startle to a bike horn, use sounds of less intensity to elicit an eye blink (for example, loud shakers or a drum).

- Finally, the child does not smile at this level but will often cry or whine. This makes it hard for everyone. Often stimulation therapy briefly interrupts crying. Don't hesitate to hold or have parents hold their child at this level for stimulation therapy.

## Level 3: A Localized Response

The child at this level demonstrates a localized response to sensory stimuli. This means the child has the ability to localize sound, track visually, focus, and move in response to stimulation.

Often the child will begin to smile at this stage, which is incredibly joyful for everyone and provides crucial feedback about what the child enjoys in therapy.

The goals at Level 3 are (1) to elicit responses to sensory input of less intensity, (2) elicit and maintain attention, and (3) successfully guide the child's motor movements to adaptive activity.

### Therapy Techniques

This is the time when family photographs, picture cards, puppets, wooden form board puzzles, stacking rings, pegboards, and crib activity boards are helpful to encourage visual attention. The child does not yet comprehend language, so the child's hand is guided with puzzles, rings, and pegboards so they are successful in the activity.

The important focus is to elicit the child's ability to **pay attention to anything!** Additionally, the concept of causality—best defined as "what I do makes something happen"—begins to emerge at this level.

Because the child's motoric involvement often prevents manipulation of traditional toys, adapted switches are very useful. A switch that is easy for the child to depress is attached to various battery-operated toys: a barking dog, an electric train, a radio, a merry-go-round. The child's hand often may need to be guided on the switch but the point is to elicit the child's attention.

Many computer programs are commercially available to elicit the child's attention to visual and visual/auditory software. This is especially true when a color monitor is used and the lights in the therapy room are turned off. Many single-switch programs are very attractive visually, and most include auditory stimulation. The child's hand, once again, can easily be guided to depress the switch. The purpose of all this hand-over-hand guidance is to assist and channel the child to independent and adaptive motoric activity.

Another important consideration at this level is that parents and other family members often see responses earlier than therapists do. So don't look askance when they describe their child turning a head to Grandma's voice or visually tracking Uncle Harry. Parents are accurate in their impressions.

### Therapy Guidelines

Important considerations for conducting stimulation therapy with the Level 3 child are listed here.

- Though you should make every attempt to provide age-appropriate materials, experience has shown that teenagers at Levels 4 and 3 seem content with preschool puzzles, stacking rings, and big, colorful pictures.

  Older children are still nonresponsive to their environment linguistically and are functioning at a level of cognitive operation that is infantile. The goals of establishing cause and effect, eliciting and maintaining attention, and encouraging adaptive behavior are appropriately enhanced with colorful toys, pictures, games, and computer software.

- If agitation occurs, it will often erupt at Level 3. The child may begin to bang on the lapboard, grab hair, throw toys, cry, and pull at braces and splints. This behavior is more prevalent in physical therapy where the child is being challenged physically.

  This agitation is good—really! It means that the child is responding on a confused level to what is happening and, in the perspective of adults who have agitation following injury, it is generally easily managed and directable. Keeping the child safe is important, and therapy materials may need to be kept out of the child's immediate reach—as should your hair, jewelry, and glasses! It is rare to have to restrain a child in therapy because of agitation.

  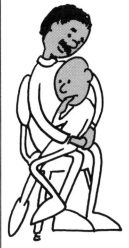

- Finally, the opportunity to soothe a child frequently goes unnoticed in any stimulation program. It is important to remember that eliciting responses is one thing, but soothing is another. It is a gentler way of providing sensory information. This is a nice opportunity for a family member to sing to a child, read familiar books, hold and rock, brush the child's hair, massage the child's face and back with warm oil, and provide tapes of lullabies and classical music.

## Stimulation Therapy: To Do or Voodoo?

For many years, actually since rehabilitation of children and adults with brain injury began, the question of what stimulation therapy does or does not do has been debated in hospital halls, rehabilitation conferences, and family living rooms. The issue under debate is whether a vigorous and intensive stimulation program improves subsequent outcome. There is some research on both sides.

A group of patients in a coma or persistent vegetative state two weeks after injury were provided a vigorous stimulation program by a relative for up to eight hours a day for seven days a week (Pierce et al. 1990).

The outcome of these patients was compared to a reference group from the literature who did not receive rigorous sensory stimulation. No difference was noted in the number of patients who emerged from coma. "This study was unable to find any evidence that coma arousal, for all its arduous

*I have often teased with my family and friends that if I am ever in a coma, I will be wearing a medical alert bracelet that states, "allergic to stimulation therapy." Instead, I would like a daily, hot oil full-body massage, shampoo of my hair, and a cassette player that plays Brahms!*

patient contacts, had a markedly better outcome compared to conventional treatment" (Pierce et al. 1990, p. 191).

Four single case studies were examined to evaluate the efficacy of a sensory stimulation protocol, where improvement was defined as change from the onset of therapy to the end (Wilson et al. 1991). All four patients showed significant changes in behavior, demonstrating increased eye opening and spontaneous movement. These cases were not matched to the literature to compare results to patients who had not received sensory stimulation.

It is important to note, however, that these studies involve adults and, to the authors' knowledge, no specific investigation of the efficacy of stimulation therapy in children has been done.

Jennett and Teasdale (1981) state that, at the very least, sensory stimulation will increase input into the reticular activating system. This might increase arousal to the threshold necessary for responsiveness in patients who are underaroused. Thus, it may seem a little more intelligent when you are tickling a child's lips at bedside to say to the doubting physician, "I am activating the reticular system." Additionally, stimulation programs allow for frequent monitoring of patients so that the ability to respond does not go unnoticed.

*I agree with the premises of Jennett and Teasdale. But perhaps on a deeper level, were one of my loved ones in a coma, I would demand an organized stimulation program to elicit responding. I have seen nonverbal, physically dependent children transferred into our program where responses to the environment and, in some cases even language, had previously gone unnoticed. These responses would have been detected within the context of a stimulation program.*

*I honestly do not believe that a stimulation program causes a child to come out of a coma. I have worked with many children who underwent an organized stimulation program and who never became able to respond to language or their environment in a meaningful way. What I think a stimulation program does is to elicit responses that may have gone unnoticed and provide external stimulation to children unable to respond to their environment on their own.*

*I would want such a program for me. I would demand one for my family.*

# Level 2:
# The Structure-Dependent
# Child

**D**id he? Was that random? Do **you** see that? **I'm** not as sure as **you** are. But can she stick out her tongue? This must be Level 2.

Level 2 is that major turning point where the child begins emerging from coma, following commands or gestured requests, and interacting purposefully with the environment.

Frequently, it is a family member who first notices the faintest movement—squeezing of a hand on request, the very edge of a tongue moving over the lip when asked, the eyes that close and are certainly more than a blink. Sometimes it is a nurse who routinely asks the child to move a foot to help with dressing and this time the foot moves! Then a therapist notices the same thing. The doctor sees it, too. This must be Level 2!

Level 2 has been described as the best cure for burnout for any medical staff or family who has persevered through Levels 4 and 3. To be there as the child is beginning to respond is truly an exciting time.

To better understand the rationale for intervention, it is important to understand the primary presenting characteristics of the child at Level 2. Consequently, this chapter first presents the symptoms of the Level 2 child, followed by the clinical and technological interventions.

## Characteristics of Level 2

Children at Level 2 display an incredible range of responsiveness, but every child at Level 2 is characterized by specific presenting symptoms: structure dependency, fatigue, confusion, memory deficits, and impaired judgment. Speech production disorders are often present and will be discussed separately.

### Structure Dependency

Structure dependency means that children are vulnerable to outside variables. They do not have any internal mechanism at this point to

motivate or monitor themselves. Children at Level 2 respond most appropriately to situations where contextual cues add a level of predictability to their world. For example, a child may not be able to pantomime how to use a spoon, but given a spoon and a dish of ice cream, would likely dig in and enjoy it very much.

Confusion is often escalated if children are asked to perform activities that require any level of listening or processing of spoken language. Thus, they need a computer, a work sheet, a puzzle, picture cards, or motor activity. Most importantly, they need **you**—right in front of their faces at all times to help orient and facilitate responding.

A calm, steady voice helps, as does simple, direct language. Avoid the tendency to talk in a *really loud voice* to try to elicit a response. Usually what results is an exhausted, irritable child. Structure and predictability—a recognizable routine—provide children with the reassurance they require.

As it relates to structure, there is little to be gained from writing a lesson plan at this level. Treatment is continually diagnostic, staying one step ahead of the child's progress. The rate of recovery at Level 2 can be very unpredictable, with some children zooming on to Level 1 within a day or two and others remaining at Level 2 for months and years. Most importantly, clinicians need to change activities many times in a half-hour session to maintain attention and facilitate responding.

### Fatigue

Fatigue is an often-overlooked symptom with children who have brain injuries, and at this level it is a common, relentless problem. The children are working to hold their heads up, pay attention, not wet, and try to speak. On top of that, everyone in the school and neighborhood is visiting. It is a wonder these children can respond at all!

The best example of this is when the child begins to talk: everyone in the hospital and family begins to demand speech: "Say 'bye'," "Say 'hi'," "What's my name?" "Count to 10," and "I love you." It is important at this point to ask everyone to go a little more slowly, but the recovery of speech is so much fun that it is difficult to resist.

The indication of fatigue in therapy is noted by what have come to be called "black holes." This is not seizure. It is a look that comes over children's faces and eyes that indicates they have mentally left the therapy session for a moment.

This is the cue to back off, stop working on the fatiguing activity (such as speech production or labeling), and change to activities where the child is more the passive recipient. This might involve telling a brief story, describing a picture, or rubbing the child's arm.

## Confusion

Confusion at this level dominates the child's every waking moment. Memory of recent events is poor and the child cannot recall who these therapists are, remember what was done yesterday, or predict what might be done next. Parents need to be counseled to expect memory problems and the resultant confusion. Encourage parents not to be alarmed if the child has no recall of Grandma's visit, or the fact the child is in the hospital. For the most part, as the child's memory improves, confusion will decrease.

If a child at Level 2 is talking, the conversation frequently reflects the confusion. Older children may spin tall tales, a process called confabulation. It is not deliberate on the child's part but is the mind's way of accounting for this confusion. For example, the child may tell people he/she is at a hotel, or the therapist may remind the child of "Auntie Carole," and will call her that. As the child's memory improves, confabulation becomes less evident.

It is important to understand that confusion and anxiety generally are reflections of the child's memory difficulties.

## Memory

On a practical level, there are three types of memory to consider.

*Remote memory* refers to the child's recall of events before the accident: for example, what was gotten for a birthday present, a school teacher's name, a family vacation, or the name of a pet. These are the memories that are stored prior to the child's accident. They are usually retrievable unless the child suffers complete post-traumatic amnesia.

Sometimes it is confusing when a child is able to recall an incident from a year ago but cannot remember what happened the day before. However, a brain injury interrupts the storage of new information and may have limited impact on recall of previously stored information.

*Recent memory* is the most vulnerable to traumatic brain injury. It refers to the child's recall of recent events: what happened yesterday, an hour ago, 15 minutes ago, and in some cases, three to five minutes ago.

*Immediate memory* refers to the child's ability to recall what just happened or what was just said, generally within the span of one to two minutes.

A child's ability to pay attention, the level of fatigue, and distractibility directly influence the child's immediate memory. How the child perceives and processes information dictates whether that information can be stored at all and, most importantly, retrieved as recent or remote information.

The consequences of memory problems and remediation strategies will be discussed throughout the intervention sections of this book.

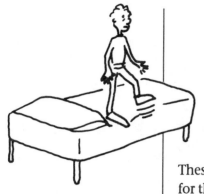

## Impaired Judgment

Another primary characteristic of Level 2 is impaired judgment. Children at this level do not have the ability to make a safe decision. The part of the brain that helps to weigh the consequences of their actions has been impaired. So if they decide to stand and walk, they just do it. Reminders that this sort of thing is dangerous have little impact, because of their poor memory.

These children need constant supervision, and decisions must be made for them. Many times they do not have the organizational skills to initiate an activity and, once begun, they frequently don't know how to stop or discontinue the activity without external cuing or physical prompting. Most children at this level are restrained in their wheelchairs due to the impulsivity.

## Speech and Language Disorders

It is important to discuss the speech and language characteristics of these children.

### Aphasia

If the centers for language have been injured, the child may experience what is called dysphasia or aphasia. This is the disruption of the under-standing of spoken or written communication and a reduced ability to name familiar things or speak in sentences. These difficulties are also present in the child who has memory problems or who is confused. Consequently, a clear diagnosis cannot always be made until the child is at Level 1.

### Flat Affect

A second speech characteristic may be a "flat affect," best described as lack of facial expression, a monotone voice, and lack of emotional response. This frequently happens when the front portion or the right side of the brain has been involved in the injury. Children with this type of injury may also fail to recognize these characteristics in others. They don't seem to recognize frustration, excitement, or subtle facial expressions.

If the child has muscle weakness of the face and mouth, flat affect can be even more exaggerated. These changes in the child's personality can be very discouraging to the family, but they also improve with the child's recovery. Specific therapy suggestions will be presented in Chapter 9, which describes Level 1.

### Dysarthria and Apraxia

Dysarthria and apraxia occur frequently at this level, and both sets of symptoms may be present in the speech of the Level 2 child.

**Dysarthria.** Dysarthria is considered to be an overall muscle weakness caused by injury to the part of the brain that controls the muscles of speech. This includes the trunk muscles that assist in breath support and the muscles of the larynx, the soft palate, the tongue, the cheeks, and the lips.

Dysarthria may result from cortical injury to the motor strip or injury to the cranial nerves. Speech of the child with dysarthria is sometimes weak, breathy, and slurred.

**Apraxia.** The causes of apraxia are somewhat more difficult to understand. It is apparently caused by injury to the part of the brain that helps to plan muscle movements. Children with apraxia seem to struggle to start speech, or they say a word with the sounds turned around (for example, "carps" for "scarf," or "pappo" for "apple").

Many doctors and therapists refer to "motor planning difficulties." Usually, children with this type of disorder can recite a nursery rhyme much better than they can spontaneously carry on a conversation.

In cases of a more severe apraxia, the child might seem to be speaking nonsense (referred to as "jargon"). In fact, many of these children can speak quite fluently when asked to talk nonsense. Their intonation and melody patterns are often preserved and are more evident when they are encouraged to talk silly or nonsense talk.

It is not unusual for a child to demonstrate more than one or all of these speech and language characteristics due to the diffuse nature of severe brain injuries.

This has been a basic introduction to the behaviors and characteristics observed in the Level 2 child. It is important to remember that everything the children do—or don't do—is reflective of their cognitive dysfunction. Consequently, the therapeutic approach at this level is in direct response to their extreme structure dependency. Keep that in mind as some of the remediation strategies are discussed in the following section.

# Therapy

Therapy at Level 2 should follow the guidelines listed here.

1. Provide maximum structure to elicit the child's highest level of response.

2. Enlist the assistance of the family to provide the most familiar, meaningful stimuli.

3. Be flexible and continually evaluate to match the child's rapidly changing and fluctuating cognitive status.

*The materials and activities we use are dictated by the age and the needs of the child. With a younger child we would use large, soft, colorful blocks that can be manipulated; with teens, we might use colorful, familiar magazine pictures.*

*If a child is demonstrating obvious visual difficulties, it is generally more effective to use objects rather than two-dimensional drawings. A tape-recorded song or environmental noises may be more soothing to children who become threatened or agitated when objects are placed in front of them.*

*We have found no magical set of materials that are the "key" to cognitive retraining. We resort to anything we can to reach the child's attention.*

Specific therapy goals include:

- continued orientation to reality
- assessment and facilitation of speech production
- administration of baseline language measures
- assessment and facilitation of recent memory skills
- facilitation of increased attention to task
- facilitation of organization of language and thought

## Orientation

One of the earliest activities at Level 2 is to orient the child. Unlike adults and the typical questions asked to orient them, the child is not expected to know the name of the president of the United States. Rather, start with more familiar, recognizable biographical information. Questions such as "Are you a girl?" "Do you have any brothers?" "Do you eat dirt?" are much more likely to elicit a response.

As the child becomes more aware of the surroundings, questions such as "Have you seen me before?" or "Are you in school?" are a gentle way of beginning to orient the child to the present situation.

Orientation is a process that is repeated over and over. Remember, these children frequently cannot recall information that has been presented only a minute or two before. It is important to reintroduce yourself and repeat why the child is there each session. A conversational format with an occasional question seems to be most helpful. The child shouldn't feel that this is the Grand Inquisition.

The first few moments of a session might include such statements and questions as in the following examples.

Hi, Nathan, I'm glad you came to see me again this morning. Did you have a good breakfast?

My name is Caitlin, and you come to see me every day to work on talking. You have been coming almost every day since you were in that bad car accident and had to come to the hospital.

You've been working so hard, and each day you have been a little better. We are all so proud of you. Who came with you to therapy today?

In all orientation activities, attempt to give the child an anchor in the present, whether that means pointing out that it must be summer because the child is wearing shorts, or the fact he or she is in a wheelchair, so he or she is practicing to walk again. Talk about the child's accident and the brain injury.

Keep the information simple and at their level of cognition:

Matthew, when you fell from your horse, your brain was injured. It needed a long rest, so you were asleep in a coma for two whole weeks! We kept saying "Matthew, open your eyes!" but you just kept sleeping.

But now you are starting to walk and talk again. Every day you work so hard with your therapists and nurses and Mom and Dad. We know you will be better and ready to go home soon. Can you show me what part of you got hurt when you fell off the horse?

Encourage family members to bring in photos of the family and pets. These help with remote memory and, in combination with snapshots of the child in therapy, they can assist in orienting the child to the present. Videotaping is another way to document the child's progress for the child and family. It is also a marvelous means of orienting the child.

## Communication—The Nonverbal Child

Another key area to begin to work on is speech skills. Chapter 9, describing Level 1, focuses on the more specific goals of articulation therapy. At Level 2, the therapists' and family's role is more of a facilitator to maximize the child's attempts at expressive communication.

Many children at Level 2 are still unable to use verbal communication because of dysarthria, apraxia, or a combination of the two. For some, the part of the brain that was damaged may involve the centers for language. This is dysphasia or aphasia, referred to earlier.

Regardless of the cause, children at Level 2 are frequently too cognitively disorganized and impaired in memory to use sophisticated communication devices that use computer-generated voices to talk for them. At Level 2 it is preferable to introduce the simplest means possible in re-establishing communication.

Early forms of communication might include only yes/no responses to questions. If a child is unable to coordinate movement for head nodding or shaking of the head, some children can use a thumbs-up or thumbs-down gesture. Gestures such as shoulder shrugging and facial expressions to indicate *happy, sad,* and *mad* should be encouraged.

It is not unusual for children to fail to respond to a question if they are unsure or confused. It is important to introduce the concept of "I don't know" as an acceptable response.

Note: Eye blinks have not been found to be especially helpful in communication, because all people automatically blink their eyes, and most people have very little control over that behavior.

Sometimes photographs taped to a lapboard are an effective introduction to augmentative communication. Along the same line, taped yes/no cards are helpful for some children. Many children need to be retrained to point to objects or things in the room that they might want. They don't seem to be able to organize themselves for this type of response without practice.

## Technology and Communication

With the relatively recent development of communication devices, there is sometimes a push to equip a nonverbal child with a "talking machine." For a child who is still at Level 2, this is generally not a very effective means of communication. Most are simply too confused to use the most sophisticated devices effectively.

For a few children, the introductory machines can be a somewhat helpful way to begin training the child to use a device. (These devices include the Introtalker™ by Prentke Romich, and the McCaw™ by Zygo Industries.) A voice can be recorded so that when the child presses on a picture or written word, the machine speaks words, phrases, or sentences.

A common response to this activity is that the child enjoys the voices and will activate the machine randomly without a purpose to communication. Many children simply are not able to organize themselves to initiate the use of the machine without structure or prompting. This obviously results in others guessing what the child wants to say, and then pointing to the pictures for them.

In other cases, the child finds a favorite phrase, such as "I want to go home," and then presses the same sentence over and over again.

## Speech Therapy

There are some markers to watch for that can help to indicate when to begin actual speech therapy. Usually, involuntary vocalization is heard first—laughing, coughing, crying.

Humor should never be forgotten as a magical, wonderful means to connect with the child. A silly gesture, an unexpected burp, or your own laughter may cause the child to laugh. This is sometimes the first time children hear their own voices, and it's a show-stopper when a child laughs out loud for the first time.

About the same time, the child can be encouraged to try imitation of very familiar oral motor activities. These include things such as "stick out your tongue," "blow me a kiss," "lick your lips," "Sh-Sh-Sh," and "hum me a tune."

If the child's main problem is a verbal apraxia, rote sequences and overlearned responses are sometimes effective in eliciting speech. For example, singing the ABC's, reciting a nursery rhyme, or counting to three may result in the child's first words. The primary goal for a child with verbal apraxia is to make speech a fun and comfortable experience again.

*With all of the difficulties to overcome in using communication devices, we tend to prefer to delay the use of a device until Level 1, when the child's ability to learn new information is much improved. By then, most children have begun talking, and the whole issue goes away.*

The child is likely to do much better if communication is a natural response to a situation. Confrontation naming can be an excruciating experience for the child and everyone witnessing it. However, the provision of a carrier phrase and the first sound of the word is frequently the only assistance the child needs.

Small groups may also be very beneficial in creating a normalized environment for communication. For example, nonverbal children sometimes use "hey" to gain another child's attention. Children are so in tune with peers that, if the whole group is yelling "No! No! No!" to a silly question, the nonverbal child may scream the same thing.

Once a child with verbal apraxia begins talking, progress usually occurs rather quickly. This is the child who says one or two words, and within a week or two is carrying on some simple conversation. In some cases, the only communication deficit that is obvious after several weeks is difficulty remembering particular words. This will be discussed in greater detail in Chapter 9.

There are several props that are favorites for Level 2 speech activities. Small children love to hear their voices echo and will frequently call into a hollow tube, such as an oatmeal carton or the toy silo from a toy farm set. A microphone may elicit a similar response, although just as many children want to eat the microphone.

Very familiar activities such as talking on the phone may prompt speech that is otherwise absent. Call Grandma, call Daddy at work, or call the pizza delivery man. The kids love it.

There are several computer software programs that display the children's voices on the computer monitor. These will be described in Chapter 9, a discussion of Level 1.

## Baseline Language Measures

The intertwining of language, cognition, and speech has been alluded to several times. At Level 2 it is nearly impossible to sort out completely the source of the child's communication difficulty. Understanding, expression, memory, attention, and speech are so interdependent, citing one of these as the main cause in disruption of the Level 2 child's communication would be misleading.

However, attempts should be made to measure language comprehension and usage, to help the staff and family determine the best means of interacting with the child.

A helpful standard measurement is the Peabody Picture Vocabulary Test, which measures the child's ability to identify one of four pictures as they are named. Experience indicates that what is really being measured, at times, is the child's impulsivity, poor attention, and possible visual deficits in addition to receptive vocabulary. Nonetheless, all of this does give a general indication of where the child is functioning.

If a child can name objects, the Expressive One Word Picture Vocabulary Test is also useful. Note whether the child tends to use sound substitutions as in the speech disorder described as apraxia, whether similar words (for example, calling a "pear" an "apple") are substituted, or whether nonsense words (called jargon or neologisms) are used.

The Auditory Reception subtest of the Illinois Test of Psycholinguistic Abilities is helpful on a more informal basis. The child is asked to respond "yes" or "no" to questions such as "Do bananas telephone?"

The Auditory Association subtest from that same battery assesses basic reasoning skills by asking the child to complete an open-ended sentence such as "*Up* is to *down,* as *in* is to _____." This examines the child's ability to listen and process information and draw a conclusion at very simple levels. The type of responses elicited may yield information about the child's language as well as the level of confusion.

In any case, it is always important for staff and family to view this baseline information as a temporary description of the child's language level. There is every expectation that the child's language will improve and the levels of confusion will diminish.

## Memory Assessment

Probably the most critical information that needs to be gathered relates to how affected the child's memory seems to be. Staff and family continually gather information on the child's ability to use remote, recent, and immediate memory skills. Family input is necessary for information regarding names of brothers, sisters, pets, teachers; the color of their bedroom carpeting; their favorite television show, etc.

For an obviously confused child, there are kinder and gentler means of orienting than always beginning with yes/no questions or direct questions. For example, begin with a statement such as "I bet those three sisters of yours are really missing you! Your mommy told me your big sister is Meaghan, and one of your little sisters is Becca. What is the baby's name?" Encourage families to bring in photos and memorabilia such as team trophies or favorite posters to help trigger past memories.

When introducing memory activities, try to keep the activity as age-appropriate as possible. For example, a 5-year-old wouldn't be asked to attempt number repetition. But the child might enjoy a conspiracy such as hiding someone's shoe in the filing cabinet, then within a five-minute period, asking the child to help find the lost shoe. Extend this type of activity over a 30-minute session, increasing the time as the child's memory improves.

As the child becomes increasingly alert, begin to look for signs of recognition of situations and staff. Can children point to the therapists as they are named? Do they seem to be familiar with an activity that was introduced in the morning? Do they seem to retain the steps necessary to run

*It is not uncommon for this information to be temporarily lost or confused. More than once we've asked a question such as "Do you have any sisters?" and while the child is replying "no," the parent is holding up three fingers. It is for reasons such as this that orientation and redundancy of information is so important.*

a computer program? Ask them, as some favorite materials are stored away, to remember where the things are being put so they can help find them in the afternoon.

It is important to recognize that the child's memory is interactive with other cognitive components such as attention. Therefore, goals such as "improving memory" are not exclusively geared to memory alone. A behavioral response such as sustained attention needs to be elicited along with the memory activity.

## Attention to Task

Children at Level 2 continue to experience the "black holes" referred to earlier. This phenomenon of drifting away can be pervasive. It appears to reflect the child's fatigue or complete neurological overload. Provision of structure seems to reduce the occurrences of "black holes" and allows the child to maintain attention for longer periods of time.

For the Level 2 child, "structure" refers to anything you can do to maintain and maximize attention. This may involve sitting close to the child or frequently reaching out and touching the child's arm or face. It may mean switching tasks frequently to avoid overload.

Structure may also mean lowering your expectations for the moment, or lowering the complexity of the task. For example, a Level 2 child may not respond to a command such as "Show me the doll's toes." However, the child may respond more appropriately to a situation during play where you remark, "Oh no, the baby has an owie on her toe! Kiss it!", then you place the doll's foot in an obvious position for a kiss. A child may not "point to" a particular toy but, if asked to "Put the bunny in the basket," may make an appropriate selection.

Structure does not always imply a distraction-free environment. Sometimes the addition of one or two other children or adults may heighten a child's attention and elicit more responses.

As has been noted throughout this book, humor can be used as a very effective therapy tool. If a child is struggling with reduced attention, you can maximize the child's attention for the moment by other children's laughter or by introducing an unexpected response. For example, with three children at the table, you might put a fireman's hat with a twirling light on one and a stuffed dog on another, then ask the Level 2 child to show which one is his "favorite hat." There is no correct answer; you are simply attempting to elicit attention and a response.

## The Computer and Attention

A computer and carefully selected software is an extremely useful tool for structuring responses. The computer provides a highly visible, entertaining means of engaging the child. It provides immediate feedback as the child makes choices.

Computers are easily adaptable to meet the cognitive and physical needs of the child. The single-switch activities described in Level 3 can be carried over to Level 2. As the child's cognition progresses, increase the level of difficulty to include programs that require increased attention, build in a factor of having to wait, as well as require some simple decision making.

Generally, any software that has bright, visual graphics with sound and requires a single response is acceptable for Level 2 activities. (Suggested computer programs are referenced in Appendix C.)

Adaptations such as a touch screen allow children to touch the monitor screen to make their selections. This bypasses the keyboard, which can be a major source of distraction for Level 2 children. Other adaptations (such as the PowerPad™ or the Muppet Keyboard™) allow for simplification of the keyboard and expand the keyboard for children with visual and/or physical difficulties.

A speech synthesizer is another marvelous way to capture a child's attention. It is amazing how children will focus in on the robotic-sounding voice. (Appendix C includes purchasing information for some commonly used computer peripherals.)

## Organization

The final point of discussion is how to pull all these areas of cognition together to facilitate organization of thought and language. At Level 2, this involves very basic organization. Some important components include simple sequencing, early decision making, drawing conclusions as to what could happen next, matching and discriminating differences, and how to formulate and express thoughts.

As with other therapy activities, the purpose of the activity and what needs to be done must be familiar and obvious to the child. For example, a simple dot-to-dot activity encourages attention and sequencing and, when completed, could be the basis for a naming, categorization, or descriptive activity.

Imaginary play such as a tea party provides the opportunity to discuss decisions such as "What should we put on the table first?" or "What could we serve?" A brief outing such as a trip to the snack machine affords the opportunity to plan ahead by gathering coins, scanning the machine for selections, making a choice, planning when to put the money in, and how to make the selection.

In all of these activities, it is not the activity itself that is so important, but how it is structured to meet the child's needs. The activity should exceed children's cognitive abilities just enough to cause them to concentrate on the task and think about it without overwhelming them.

## Written Organization

If a child is at a grade level where reading and writing were an established skill, you can use easy word-processing programs to assist in organization of written language. Some favorites include *Stickybear® Reading, Story Machine™*, and the *Bankstreet Writer®*. Others are referenced in Appendix C.

Asking children to compose a story about their accident reveals information regarding their memory, orientation, and organization as well as sequential thought. Keep these compositions for review and for reflecting on progress as children approach Level 1.

In closing, there are several points worth repeating. The Level 2 child's behavior reflects confusion, memory deficits, and ongoing fatigue. The cognitive status can be wildly fluctuating. These factors demand that the child receive constant supervision and structure. Therapy at this level is necessarily simplified, familiar, redundant, and highly structured. Most but not all children move through Level 2 as memory and orientation improve, eventually exhibiting those behaviors described as Level 1.

# Level 1:
# The Concrete Processor

**V**isualize the pediatric scales as widely spread rungs of a ladder. The child reaches but either does not quite achieve the rung, or overreaches, which results in slipping. Thus you can begin to appreciate the uncertainty of defining when a child is truly and *consistently* at Level 1.

As with the other levels, the child is there one moment and then slips back to Level 2 the next. So the therapist who saw the child at 9:00 worked with an alert, oriented client. By 10:30, that same child was irritable, confused, and noncommunicative.

To some, Level 1 might sound as if children have returned nearly to pre-accident status. But Level 1, while implying recovery of functional skills, is far from a full recovery. There are a vast array of behaviors that describe the Level 1 child, and as with the other levels, these behaviors reflect a progression. In the case of Level 1 it is progression from confusion (Level 2) to oriented (Level 1).

Level 1 is a stage of tremendous transition. It is a time when the rehabilitation staff and family are moving the child from acute hospitalization to home and community. It is a transition from dependence to independence. It is a transition filled with anticipation, frustration, anxiety, hope, and uncertainty. It is a level that challenges everyone professionally and personally. To describe this arduous climb, this chapter has been organized into three basic parts:

- a general description of symptoms and progress

- residual difficulties and what they mean

- suggestions for remediation

## Symptoms

"Oriented" is the key word at Level 1. Children who are oriented reflect sufficiently improved attention and recent memory to recognize their surroundings and the reason for being in the hospital. This is the point where children can describe that they were injured and perhaps even identify the consequences of the injury. As a result, they are more aware of the purpose of the therapy. That doesn't necessarily imply that they are content to be in the hospital, just more aware of why. (Insight will be discussed later in this chapter.)

At Level 1, the child recognizes routine, nurses, and therapists. These professionals are no longer strangers asking them to do pointless activities as they struggle through a fog. As a result, agitation and apprehension are less evident. Because of improvements in memory and orientation, the child is more likely to recall rules of safety. Supervision is reduced to moderate levels as increased independence is encouraged.

Some but not all of the children at Level 1 have begun to walk and talk. Most are eating orally and can, to some degree, feed and dress themselves.

It is at this point that family members feel a bit more comfortable about being gone for longer periods of time. For one reason, the children can understand that parents will be returning and when. The verbal child is now a more accurate historian of the day's activities. And finally, if the child is of school age, it is an important step in assessing the child's ability to separate from and function more independently with other adults.

While the description of the Level 1 child reflects significant improvements, it would be misleading to imply a complete recovery. Level 1 children continue to evidence many residual memory difficulties. They may be vague. They may remember the previous day's activity, but not the specifics surrounding it. They are still heavily reliant on the redundancy of a schedule or an activity to function well.

Retrieval of information is frequently faulty, so the children require cuing or prompting to recall an event. As with all cognitive functioning, memory is extremely susceptible to fatigue, stress, or just general overloading of the system.

## Attention Deficits

It is difficult to discuss memory without taking into account the child's ability to sustain attention. Cognitive skills are so heavily interdependent that a component such as compromised attention affects all other areas. Attention implies that the child is able to screen out other distractions and focus on only the pertinent information being presented, process that information, and store it away for later retrieval.

An injury to the brain disrupts this ability. Children may demonstrate brief episodes of adequate attention, but the ability to sustain attention is frequently impaired. It just requires too much energy.

## Organizational Skills

To organize, one needs to be able to prioritize, sequence steps, initiate, and proceed in an orderly fashion. These are all skills which tend to be disrupted in children with brain injury. What they see or what is most evident is generally what happens first. They are unable to analyze a situation and break it into logical steps. Many times this response goes hand in hand with their impulsivity.

### Impulsivity and Impaired Judgment

There are parts of the brain that help people to slow down and to weigh the consequences of a certain behavior. This frequently takes place in the frontal lobes. Unfortunately, this is also an area of the brain that comes into contact with the skull, particularly in accidents where there is speed involved (such as a motor vehicle or bicycle accident).

Injuries of this type result in behavior that is most often described as impulsive. Children see something and reach for it, even though it may throw them off balance. They want to get out of bed, so they do it, even though they need assistance. They see some steps, so they start climbing.

Impulsivity is not restricted to physical movement. Some of these children reflect their impulsivity in what they say. They do not have the internal mechanisms to monitor and censor what they will say next.

This reduced ability to weigh consequences is also frequently described as poor judgment. The tendency to be impulsive often leads to decisions, movements, and statements that reflect reduced judgment.

### Processing

The brain perceives, processes, and computes. When a child has received an injury to the brain, these functions are disrupted. At Level 1, these difficulties are most subtle. But there is a tendency for children at this level to process visual, auditory, and tactile information at a slower rate and to overload easily. The sensory information received by the brain may be incomplete or faulty, further compromising the child's perception or understanding of a situation.

### Egocentricity

Egocentricity is part of all children's development. Egocentric behaviors tell the rest of the world, "This is who I am, what I want, and when I want it." It is an important step in learning assertiveness.

This group of behaviors is acceptable in very young children, but it is slowly shaped into more socially acceptable requests as children grow. Children are taught to "wait" and "be patient." In time, then, children begin to demonstrate the ability to recognize the needs of others and are less focused on themselves.

A child with a recent brain injury is less inclined to perceive others' needs or to be able to read situations that call for patience or restraint. Just as impulsivity emerges, so does the drive to be first and to have needs met constantly and without delay.

External events contribute to this phenomenon as well. It is a very natural response for family, staff, and concerned others to dote on a child who has been injured, to want to make sure that all needs are met, and quickly. Much of the child's time is spent individually with adults who want to give the child their full attention, encouragement, and praise.

This is all well and good in the first stages of Level 2, but by Level 1, it is important to work toward decreasing the child's demands and increasing the tolerance for waiting.

## Pragmatic Skills

Pragmatic skills include those interactive skills that allow the child to communicate in a functional manner—to ask appropriate questions, to wait until someone has finished talking before interrupting, to maintain a conversation in a traditional manner through commenting and questioning.

Frequently at this level, children are egocentric and also present reduced or impaired pragmatic skills. Again, much of their response is a reflection of their limited perception and their increased impulsivity. They are unable to wait until someone has finished talking, or they have not been paying attention to what someone else has said, so they don't know what to say next.

There are many variations on this situation, but the result is a reduced ability to interact with others during conversation.

## Humor

Children who are recently out of coma can display a tendency toward a "flat" or "blunted" effect. In addition to this lack of facial affect, their recognition and appreciation of humor can be distorted or reduced.

The development of humor follows developmental levels (Fowles and Glanz 1976) and closely parallels the development of language and cognition (McGhee and Goldstein 1983).

> Children as well as adults are most likely to appreciate humor that is at or just above their cognitive level (Zigler and Levine 1967). Children with brain injuries tend to process verbal humor at slower rates and with poor recognition of the language subtleties. As a result, their recognition of humor is less mature than it was before the accident.

Most people have experienced that uncomfortable moment when they can't remember the punch line, or when everyone else seems to "get it" and they don't. All too often, this is the position in which these children find themselves.

Misplaced or inappropriate use of humor, while briefly entertaining, can eventually become annoying. This, too, often leads to difficulty in interacting with others.

## Residual Speech Deficits

Most but not all children are speaking by the time they reach Level 1. Verbal apraxia is generally less plaguing at this point, although it may not be completely resolved. More commonly, flat affect, facial hemiparesis, and dysarthria are the residual speech difficulties.

Occasionally, there are children who have cognitively reached Level 1 but who still have severe apraxias and/or dysarthria and whose speech remains unintelligible. Considerations for augmentative communication will be discussed in the intervention section of this chapter.

This list of symptoms is a collective list of behaviors and does not apply to all children at Level 1. Nor do children at Level 1 display all of these behaviors.

Such a long list of "inabilities, difficulties, and deficits" tends to give the impression of pessimism. This is certainly not the intention. Rather, this is meant to be a general description to provide a framework for remediation strategies. The important "positive" to take from this chapter is that the children are oriented. Memory is improving. Learning is taking place.

# Therapy Goals

At Level 1, the children's underlying cognitive dysfunction must always be taken into account when formulating goals and procedures.

For most children, there are five main areas which require focused attention.

1. Continue to facilitate immediate and recent memory. Children need to be using their emerging memory for recall of daily events and learning new information.

2. Facilitate those cognitive skills that enhance effective use of language (such as discrimination, classification, conceptualization, problem solving, and inference).

3. Increase independent functioning in a less structured, more demanding environment. The goal here is to carefully but deliberately peel away the structure that was so important at Level 2 and allow for increased independent decision making.

4. Continue to assess and refine speech and/or nonspeech communication skills.

5. Promote improved communication as a social tool and move beyond concrete functioning.

None of these skills is mutually exclusive. The main goal at this level is integration of cognitive skills. Consequently, there is deliberate redundancy and overlap of goals. To be effective, all goals must be transdisciplinary.

# Activities and Procedures

Activities and procedures are suggested as general guidelines rather than a step-by-step approach to therapy. In establishing goals, each child and family will have unique characteristics and needs that should influence the priority and weighing of goals.

For the most part, activities are interdependent on the child's level of physical and cognitive recovery. So, for example, a chosen memory activity will also require increased attention on the child's part. An activity such as puzzle completion is influenced by the child's visual and motor skills as well as attention, organizational abilities, and so on.

## Memory

Immediate memory activities are easily structured and easily measured. Introduce familiar activities such as Concentration or Memory. It is easy to control the variables (such as the number of cards that are used, the types of pictures, and the way they are displayed).

The children's styles or strategies also give information about attention levels and problem-solving skills. For example, do they explore the possibilities by turning over cards in various locations, or do they tend to persist with one or two cards? When they have the possibility of a match, do they use a strategy to locate the match, or impulsively turn over the card they have just seen? Do they remember to wait their turn?

There are numbers of software manufacturers that include concentration boards or memory games in their activities. The Sunburst Corporation referenced in Appendix C has developed a series of memory activities that span kindergarten through elementary school levels.

An example of this type of activity is Memory Castle™, which incorporates several cognitive activities. The child is asked to store and retrieve information in sequential order. The number of directions to be recalled can be varied by the therapist.

Some children may need to be encouraged to write down each step. Others may require only one or two key words. For a more advanced activity, the child might be encouraged to visualize the steps, tell a story to increase retention, and then recall the steps without written prompts.

Auditory memory activities are the focus of many workbook activities and are referenced in Appendix C. These are often presented in the form of a sentence or paragraph that is read to the child and is followed by some questions. For many children, it is important to provide visual props such as pictures or objects. When physically able, children might act out or role play a story to increase attention and recall.

## Recent Memory

One important and functional way to evaluate memory is to challenge recent memory. Subtly assess how the child is recalling the previous day's events. Ask the child, for example, to put away a game. During the following session, start by saying, "Stephanie, I can't remember where I asked you to put Animal Lotto. Can you help me find it?" Then, as an assignment, you can remark, "Now tomorrow, you are in charge of finding this game. Don't forget!"

An extremely valuable tool is the instant camera. Ask parents to photograph weekend activities as reminders and therapy materials for the following week.

## Log Book

For older children, a log book can be used effectively to help record a day's activities. Writing things down helps in the storage process and is available for reference if retrieval of information is faulty. It also provides nurses and therapists with cues to help elicit the information. You might notice, for example, "Oh, I see in Therapeutic Rec. that you went to the gift shop. What did you buy there?"

## Humor

The use of humor has been shown to improve attention, facilitate learning, and aid in storage and retrieval of information (Zillman et al. 1980). Telling children a simple knock-knock joke and asking them to share it the next day reveals a good deal about their language comprehension and usage as well as their recent memory skills.

*As firm believers in the benefit of humor in healing and recovery, we incorporate jokes, riddles, puns, and visual humor in daily therapy activities.*

## Cognitive Skills

Cognition is knowing through perceiving. Cognitive skills are the underlying processes that allow people to look at the "whole picture" and break it down to smaller parts or sequences, or to look at the smaller pieces and figure out how to put them together in a logical fashion to make something whole.

Frequently, educators will list cognitive skills as the ability to discriminate, classify, conceptualize, problem solve, and infer. For the purpose of this section, cognitive skills are defined as those thinking processes that allow children to function safely and independently and to learn new information.

It is these complex, interrelated thinking skills that are so easily disrupted by illness and fatigue. Most people have experienced that feeling of being too tired to "think straight." In even very mild brain injuries, it is the subtle aspects of cognition that so often continue to be problematic.

## Computer Activities

Throughout the therapy sections of this book, use of the computer has been encouraged. At Level 1, it is an invaluable tool for cognitive activities. It would be futile to list all the useful software that is available. The following descriptions provide a basic idea of the types of activities to choose for a child who is functioning at Level 1.

There is a tremendous amount of software that requires the child's attention to visual detail. Factory™ by Sunburst/WINGS for Learning is an excellent example of incorporating numbers of cognitive skills to produce a product. The child needs to visually analyze a "product" that is "manufactured" and then select a number of machines to duplicate the process. The machines must be chosen in a particular sequence to achieve the correct effect. This is a structured, non-threatening means of focusing the child's attention to detail, sequence, and attributes of an object.

Groups such as The Learning Company have developed series of activities that encourage sorting, classification, and organizational skills. Many of these programs are developed for different age levels. For example, *Gertrude's Secrets*® builds thinking skills for 3- to 7-year-olds, while *Think Quick!*® is designed for 7- to 14-year-olds.

The Minnesota Educational Computer Corporation also produces some excellent programs that draw on problem-solving strategies.

In *The Oregon Trail*™, the child is given a budget and many decisions to make in order to travel from Minnesota to Oregon by covered wagon. The child must consider weather, food, illness, and hostile individuals. Again, this is a fun way to challenge children's thinking and to assist them in examining the consequences of their decisions.

*Zoyon Patrol*™ is a rather involved program for older children. It encourages deductive reasoning skills through gathering information, categorizing, and inferring information.

The *Carmen Sandiego*® series from Brøderbund were designed originally for history and geography classes. However, they are also terrific to teach problem-solving strategies and deductive reasoning. They are particularly fun for adolescent groups.

## Workbooks

Workbooks have traditionally provided activities that facilitate categorization, association, and discrimination. Susan Brubaker and others have published many creative activities.

The MEER manual by LinguiSystems also provides some challenging questions. Some favorites involve twists on traditional thinking. For example, asking children to "Name something that is *not* red" forces them to think a bit more flexibly. Asking children to tell you something they "would not say in a restaurant" requires that they first think about what people say, and then identify what is not appropriate to say and why. Another favorite is to describe a situation: "The man's clothes were all wet. What might have happened?"

For all activities, the important goal is to encourage flexible, divergent thinking.

## Written Language

Written activities work well to facilitate expressive language as well as organization. Written language encompasses handwriting, computer activities such as word processing, and some of the early writing programs such as *Story Machine*™.

Written activities are also a means of building independent skills for future classroom participation.

Frequently, the more open-ended these assignments are, the more concrete the children are in their responses. For example, when Jim was asked to define "robin," he responded, "A robin has two colors; brown on brown with light brown on his chest."

To help with organization, many of the workbook activities provide worksheets. A typical activity might include sentences with omitted words. The child needs to infer a response and fill in the blank. At a more challenging level, the activity begins with a phrase and asks the child to complete the sentence. A particularly difficult challenge is to formulate a written paragraph, a formidable task for many people but even more so for the child with brain injury.

Much of the children's written language reflects tangential thinking. This letter from a former patient displays this clearly.

> I get comments all the time on that booklet you guys made me I really miss you guys. Mom was really surprised that I remembered so much on the computer. My aunt and uncle have one and they use it for their income tax and stuff like that. Well (that's a deep hole in the ground with water in it but if you're lucky it's got oil). Have a Merry Christmas and a Happy New Year. Oh back to the computer they have a game that I played. Love you both.

Another very structured tool for older children is to begin early introduction of simple word-processing programs. The use of an outline encourages increased organization and sequential thought. Once the framework is established, it is easier for the child to remain on topic and elaborate ideas in a more systematic way.

## Increased Independent Functioning

The best means of assessing children's readiness for increased independence is simply to give them some. When appropriate, request that the children keep track of their schedules, sign out to therapy, and get themselves where they belong and on time.

Obviously, there are many small steps that are taken while that child is being supervised. For example, at a hallway intersection, you might ask the child to direct the way. At the completion of a therapy session, ask, "Where do you go next?" "Who will you see there?" If a child's primary mobility is a wheelchair, begin training them to navigate the hallway.

It is also important to know if the children can structure their own time effectively. To do this, assign older children homework to be completed on the unit, or ask them to schedule independent computer time. How children complete these types of activities is one of the primary indicators of their readiness to return to home and school.

## Speech Production

With an occasional exception, most children at Level 1 have speech as their primary means of communication. However, many still evidence the flat affect and/or dysarthria described at Level 2. Some may remain apraxic as well, although this is less common. At Level 1, therapists are better able to focus on these residual difficulties because of the improved attention and awareness of the child.

## Flat Affect

The way people express themselves is dependent on more than just speech. Body posture, facial expressions, and the gestures used all contribute to the message. Equally important are the intonation patterns and emphasis placed on certain words. Depending on the nature of the injury, any or all of these very important parts of communication can be altered.

Frequently, what has been described as flat affect continues, even though speech skills may be quite intelligible. These are the children who seem to lack emotion in their speech. The rate and prosody of speech may be affected, resulting in a monotone. Even though these children *feel* emotion, they cannot always show it.

Group settings are useful for children to provide feedback to each other regarding their speech. Also helpful is role playing that requires emphasis on particular words or facial expressions to convey the true meaning of the message.

There are some commercially available materials, such as *Communicate*® by Thinking Publications, that facilitate group discussions and highlight the importance of increased expression.

Videotaping these types of activities greatly increases feedback to the children and heightens their insight as to how to improve their interactions.

Most children show improvement in these areas over time. But it is a very slow, subtle change. One of the greatest sources of frustration is that, due to the nature of their injuries, the children themselves often cannot detect the differences. This may result from right hemisphere damage. The right hemisphere is usually the part of the brain that assists in recognizing and using melody and intonation patterns.

Another factor may be diminished insight and attention to those features that are less obvious. Whatever the underlying cause, the result is an elusive area for remediation.

Over the last several years, computer software that displays voices on the monitor have become increasingly entertaining and are generally very easy to use. The SpeechViewer™ by IBM is a particularly enjoyable program and is a very good adjunct to traditional articulation therapy. It lights up a clown's nose with increased intensity. Monkeys climb trees as the children attempt to match vowel productions, and trains chug on tracks as the children work on increased breath support and sustained vocalization. It certainly beats articulation drills!

## Technology

In discussing the nonverbal child and technology at Level 2, it was pointed out that difficulties with memory and confusion often preclude the use of sophisticated electronic devices. While memory has improved and confusion has diminished at Level 1, cognitive deficits continue to present major stumbling blocks to successful use of augmentative communication systems.

There are children who are able to use augmentative communication devices successfully. They are the children with extremely severe dysarthria but less cognitive involvement. For this group, careful evaluation of communication needs, physical abilities, and visual perceptual skills is critical. And always, always, always take into consideration their cognitive abilities.

It is very easy to fall into the trap of purchasing a device without careful consideration of all of these factors. The best answer is to use the computer and adapted keyboards to further evaluate the child's attention, vigilance, and physical abilities prior to recommending a device. Most companies provide a rental period with a device, a very wise step to take before actually purchasing the device.

*Currently, we have not found an electronic device that allows for patients' cognitive deficits and still meets their communicative needs.*

*Groups can also provide socialization and peer support. Being located in a children's hospital provides us with the luxury of bringing children with a variety of diagnoses together for group activities. It's amazing how the kids love to tell their stories over and over again to peers—and how supportive they can be to each other's needs. They truly learn a lot from each other—and we from them.*

## Communication—A Social Tool

Lastly, and perhaps most importantly, it is necessary to promote communication as a social tool. Humor, social perception, verbal turn-taking, and insight are essential components to social survival.

Unfortunately for children who demonstrate slower processing skills, reduced ability to express themselves, and egocentric thinking, these are pretty elusive skills. Children with brain injuries have been referred to as passing rehabilitation but failing life.

If the goal is to increase social communication, it is critical to provide a social situation. Ideally, these skills are worked on in small groups. Not only do groups provide a forum for practicing conversation, they also provide a means of assessing the child's ability to function in a less structured setting that begins to simulate a classroom environment.

Group activities are chosen according to the general needs and goals of the group. If the goal is to provide language activities, reference workbooks and games such as *Family Feud*™ (Pressman Toy Corporation, New York), *Trivial Pursuit*® (Horn Abbot Ltd./Parker Brothers, Beverly, Massachusetts), and password-type games work well. If the focus is on memory and attention, Bingo, Concentration, phone orders, and activities such as story completion are used.

The group also serves as a forum for humor. The kids love to be videotaped while role-playing, telling jokes, and providing puns and riddles. Humor at this level is not sophisticated, just fun.

L evel 1 is a functional but incomplete recovery. Children at Level 1 are oriented, have functional memory, and are continuing to learn. However, their thinking skills remain at concrete levels and are susceptible to overload and fatigue. Level 1 is where the bridge from hospital to home and school is begun. Chapter 11 discusses the transition from the acute setting to the child's community.

# Feeding:
# The Inside Story

● ● ● ● ●

Eating. It occupies our minds most of our waking day—and for some of us, even in our sleep. Food ads fill our magazines, our billboards, our TVs. We are told what to eat, what not to eat, and how to eat it—quickly, slowly, raw, charred, with fingers, or without—but always with our mouths closed.

Our society has taken a basic human need—nourishment—and turned it into one big, sleek, attractive advertisement. From nearly the moment of our first breath, we have all been encouraged to eat. Being fed or eating has connected us to our caregivers, whether they were parents, grandparents, day-care providers, or teachers.

It is no wonder, then, that when children are seriously injured and cannot be nourished through ordinary means, families and the rehabilitative team are focused on what the options are and how soon oral feeding can be resumed.

● ● ● ● ●

## Nonoral Feedings

Many children in the first stages of their recovery are receiving calories through intravenous or nasogastric feedings. These are necessary because the children are not alert enough to take food by mouth, or the muscles of the face, mouth, and neck are not coordinated enough to swallow safely or effectively. As a result, there is a high risk that they might choke or aspirate food into the trachea and lungs, which can lead to pneumonia.

*Our experience is that many of these children will learn to eat safely. Our job is to figure out when, where, and how.*

# Oral Feeding

There are many good reasons to pursue oral feeding for children, even though they may be regaining consciousness at a very slow rate:

- It is one of the best forms of stimulation. It is familiar and involves the senses of smell, touch, and taste.

- If oral stimulation is not provided to some children, they forget what it is like to have food in their mouths, and they find it to be an unpleasant feeling later when feeding is attempted. Oral defensiveness is sometimes one of the major stumbling blocks to orally feeding children following traumatic brain injury.

- Oral feeding re-establishes bonds with others. Nourishing and nurturing go hand in hand. People are more likely to talk and interact with a child they are feeding orally, or to hold a baby while giving a bottle.

- Feeding is an area where the family can be the therapist. It gives them something very important that they can be doing to help their child.

However, there are some important decisions that must be made before a child can be fed by mouth. The first is how the child will be nourished while relearning to eat. If it will be more than a few weeks, some children do better with a temporary gastrostomy.

This allows the medical team to remove the nasogastric tube. An NG tube is a good means of temporarily sustaining a child, but it can irritate the nose and becomes a frequent target for a child's hand. Many children have become masters at yanking out NG tubes. They overcome obstacles that would have stymied Houdini!

# Reflux

Some children have significant muscle weakness or poor coordination of the stomach muscles. This can cause the contents of the stomach to splash back out into the esophagus. This is called *reflux* and can create a severe burning similar to heartburn.

Children with this problem frequently cry after being fed, can become quite rigid, and generally look uncomfortable. If reflux is suspected, the doctor may ask for a specific test to confirm whether this is a possibility.

If reflux is confirmed, the surgeon may use a procedure called a Nissen fundoplication to keep the stomach contents contained in the stomach during digestion. This operation is frequently done at the same time as the gastrostomy.

# The Feeding Team

Once the child's nutritional needs can be met routinely and the child is comfortable, the rehabilitation team and the family can begin to focus on goals for feeding the child by mouth.

A feeding team has many members: child, family, nurse, speech-language pathologist, occupational therapist, physician, nutritionist, and radiologist. The input from all of these people is important as decisions are being made. With some children, there are "windows of opportunity" for feeding. A child needs to be alert enough to participate but cannot be safely fed when agitated, resistant, or unhappy.

# Readiness

There are some milestones that are important in progressing toward oral feeding. The child needs to be well positioned. Sometimes this might require positioning in a wheelchair. Children need to be able to hold their heads fairly well or have a head support of some kind that helps them keep the head up.

If children are sitting up well, they need to be monitored to see if they routinely drool or if they are swallowing regularly. It is important to check for muscle weakness or poor coordination of the face or mouth. This can best be done during oral stimulation activities.

Chapter 7 included a discussion of stimulation at Levels 4 and 3. Those same materials and techniques are appropriate here. Disposable toothbrushes soaked with flavors encourage the child to salivate. Swab the child's mouth and lips with the flavor, then gently close the child's mouth and place two fingers at the top of the neck to feel for a swallow. If there is no swallow, gentle stroking from the chin to the neck sometimes triggers a swallow.

Take note of how long it takes the child to swallow. If the child is unhappy or resists during these activities, they should be performed briefly but every day until the child seems more comfortable with the taste and touch. Other important activities include the use of smells in stimulation therapy, discussed in Chapter 7.

If biting down on things is not a problem, frozen pops, suckers, and frozen licorice can be used as more interesting items. Watch for anticipation. Do the children look at the food? Do they open their mouth as you approach? Frequently, children may appear very confused and disorganized as you put things in their mouth. Over time, this should decrease.

# Videofluoroscopy

A critical step is the point at which the team feels a videofluoroscopy can be done. This is usually a judgment call. To do an effective study, the child must be positioned well in a very small area. If a child is agitated, crying, or cannot be securely positioned, the study should be postponed. However, a child should never be considered safe to feed until a videofluoroscopic study has been completed.

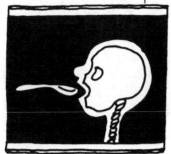

Many children aspirate without obvious coughing or choking. The only way to be reasonably sure the child is swallowing safely and to rule out silent aspiration is to perform a videofluoroscopic study. It is simply an X-ray that is done while a child is eating and drinking. During that time, a videotape is made of the X-ray so the speech-language pathologist and the radiologist can review how the child is using the lips and tongue to chew and swallow.

Observations are made as to the time it takes for the child to form a bolus of food and move it to the back of the tongue. This usually triggers a swallow reflex. If the muscles are strong and coordinated enough, the food is propelled into the esophagus and eventually to the stomach.

If there is dysfunction, such as cranial nerve involvement, food may trickle over the back of the tongue and spill into the trachea. In other instances, the larynx or the epiglottis cannot close quickly or sufficiently enough to protect the airway satisfactorily. If this happens, the child aspirates and is not ready to be fed by mouth.

Some children can handle pureed fruits and vegetables and even chopped foods because of the increased texture. This gives them more sensation and allows the tongue more time to prepare for swallowing. But the same child who can handle these foods may not be able to do as well with liquids because they trickle too quickly. These children may still be fed safely if the liquids are thickened.

# Thickening Agents

Some recommended thickening agents include applesauce, baby rice cereal, gelatins, puddings, and crushed soda crackers. Commercial products such as Nutrathick (Bruce Medical Supply, 411 Waverly Oaks Road, Apt. 10242, Waltham, MA, 02154) and Thick-It (Milani Foods, Inc., 2525 Armitage Ave., Melrose Park, IL, 60160) are also available.

# A Feeding Program

Oral feeding should be introduced slowly with a few chosen team members. This usually includes the family, the primary nurse, and the speech-language pathologist. In some settings, the occupational therapist is the primary feeder. In any instance, it is important for one person to oversee the feeding program and to make sure that only those people who are informed and trained are feeding the child.

Initially, small amounts are given. If necessary, traditional facilitation techniques such as supported lip closure and stroking under the chin to encourage swallowing can be used.

Calorie counts are implemented once the child is taking more than a cup or two of food daily. Then the nutritionist, the nurse, and the physician can begin to look at reducing the amount of calories that are given through tube feedings. This helps to increase the child's appetite and interest in eating.

A careful balancing routine is maintained until it is clear that the child is taking enough food by mouth to remain healthy. Many times the decision is made to keep the gastrostomy in for a period of time to see the child through illnesses. Or if it takes a very long time for the child to eat, the gastrostomy can be used to make sure the child receives adequate nutrition.

Some children are able to take solids by mouth and receive additional fluids and medications through their gastrostomies. Eventually, many gastrostomies can be reversed.

# Other Issues

Once children can handle the overall mechanisms of eating fairly well, there are still issues to keep in mind.

Many Americans demonstrate limited judgment when it comes to eating. Bites are too big—people "stuff their faces." These characteristics are even more prevalent in children with cognitive impairments. Kids can be impulsive, eating too quickly, or swallowing before they have adequately chewed the food.

Because children can also be distracted by everyone and everything, meals can be a very disorganized affair. Many children do better with a structured time for eating and always with adult supervision.

Some children have visual difficulties, such as field cuts, which result in an inability to see the entire visual field. For this reason, the food may need to be placed in front of the children one item at a time and in a spot they can easily see.

Adapted equipment as recommended by an occupational therapist may be needed to allow for the child to begin to eat more independently.

# Weight Gain

More than occasionally, weight gain becomes an eventual concern. Some children do not seem to recognize when they are truly hungry or when they are full, perhaps because of the part of the brain that was damaged.

Other children seem to be easily bored or are restricted in their activities. The human response is to eat more.

It is also predictable that well-meaning visitors will arrive with a vast array of goodies that are frequently consumed in excessive amounts. The result is children who are launched into a cycle of weight gain, reduced physical activity, and more eating. It is important to introduce a balanced and reasonable diet from the beginning, as hard as that may be.

# Continued Hope

For those children who continue to have gastrostomies, there is still hope that they will take some food by mouth. Continued oral stimulation is encouraged as part of a comprehensive stimulation program. Repeat videofluoroscopic studies are almost always recommended before a child is progressed to eating orally.

The following summarizes the important points of this chapter:

- Children may require an alternative means of being fed during the early stages of their recovery.

- Children can be fed once a videofluoroscopy shows that they are swallowing safely.

- Oral feeding is a good form of stimulation. If a child cannot be fed by mouth, an oral stimulation program should be continued. Such a child may relearn to eat at a later time.

- Children with brain injuries need to be supervised during meals. Their diet and eating habits place them at risk for rapid weight gain.

- Food and eating connect people. They are a vital part of the child's and family's rehabilitation. A carefully implemented feeding program will be an important first step for children who can eventually eat, drink, and be merry.

# Discharging the Child from Acute Rehabilitation: The Continuum of Care

**D**ischarge! Any way you say it, this word causes trembling and trepidation in the family! The acute hospital became a comfortable place, then the acute rehabilitation center became comfortable, and now the community receives the charge to care for this child with a brain injury in such a way as to continue to maximize recovery. The community must care for the family also. This is a scary time for the family—never underestimate it!

This fear is always just a little surprising, considering that the child has been home on numerous passes by now and the family is well instructed in the child's care. Yet many mothers have reported that it is very much like taking an infant home from the hospital, only a thousand times worse! All the feelings of inadequacy arise and parents begin to doubt their abilities.

Additionally, families are introduced to the arena of special education and other community resources. This is all new to families, and of course there is the understandable concern and fear that their child's return to school will be unpleasant.

The most important thing to remember at discharge is to tell families that discharge from the acute rehabilitation hospital is **not the end** of a child's recovery from brain injury. Children do keep getting better after discharge.

## When Discharge Happens

Children are discharged under two basic categories: (1) those who are at Levels 4 and 3, whose slow rate of progress does not warrant in-patient intensive therapies; and (2) those who are discharged at Levels 2 and 1, whose physical recovery has reached the point where they don't need twice-daily physical and occupational therapy. The priority shifts then from the child's physical status to educational and social parameters.

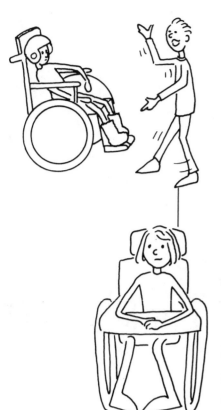

In our experience, one-fourth of children are discharged cognitively and physically dependent (Levels 4 and 3), and three-fourths recover the ability to walk, talk, and care for themselves.

This chapter will be organized under those two scenarios: discharge of the functionally comatose child, and discharge of the child at Level 2 or 1.

# Discharge of the Functionally Comatose Child

This is the child who leaves the hospital cognitively and physically dependent. These children are referred to as functionally comatose, which means that they are not responding to language and cannot interact purposefully with their environment.

A much more emotionally explosive term is *persistent vegetative state*. This term was originally introduced by Jennett and Plum (1972) to describe those patients with irreversible brain damage who pass into a stage of seeming wakefulness and reflex responsiveness but do not return to a cognitive state.

This term has become one of popular usage particularly in contemporary society's struggle to determine what is ethically appropriate in the treatment of these people. The term *vegetative* simply refers to the fact that functions at the brain stem level (breathing, circulation, and feeding) are preserved. These patients may have a feeding tube but they are able to breathe without a respirator.

Following brain injury, most children pass through this stage where they have minimal arousal to maximal stimulation. Fortunately, the majority move beyond this stage but, as mentioned previously, some do not and they are discharged from the hospital in that condition.

It is certainly premature to classify a child as in a persistent vegetative state just a few months after the injury. On the unfortunate side of recovery, some of these children do remain unresponsive to language or their environment while others, on the more fortunate side, do eventually respond. There have been children who eventually became able to walk and talk. Chapter 12, Current Research, includes a description of long-term outcome studies for children with brain injuries.

Whatever the outcome, it is a sad time indeed when children are discharged in a state of total dependency. It is sad for the family and it is sad to those in acute rehabilitation also who shared the family's hope for recovery on admission and through the hospital stay.

There are always numerous steps to discharge the child successfully at this level.

## The Responsibility

*I feel very uncomfortable discussing the discharge of the child at Levels 4 and 3 because the role of speech-language pathologists is minor compared to other members of the team. For example, the physical therapist is responsible for fitting the child in the best available equipment to optimize recovery and provide a safe seating system. Additionally, the physical therapist helps the family choose a safe car transportation system.*

*The occupational therapist is responsible for bath equipment, and both therapy professionals help the family understand their home in the new light of a wheelchair and other equipment.*

*The social worker helps the family sift through the nightmare of social system paperwork which includes Social Security Disability, TEFRA, insurance funding parameters, and of course the new arena of special education.*

*The rehabilitation nurse is invaluable in teaching the family to care for their child. This is an impressive task, and repeatedly, I have seen families learn to suction their child, give tube feedings, and properly position the child. Some of these children have in-home nursing care after discharge and thus our staff nurses instruct the home health care nurses about care of the child.*

*Certainly the rehabilitation physician is important in coordinating the discharge process and communicating with insurance and community agencies to ensure that the most comprehensive, supportive care is made available.*

## Categories of Discharge

Functionally comatose children are generally discharged to three settings: home and the community school, residential placement, and foster homes.

Most children from the program with which the authors are familiar go home. In fact, close to 85% of children discharged at Levels 4 and 3 do go home. Not uncommonly, these children have supportive nursing care in the home. Additionally, if they are school age, they attend classes for children with mental and physical disabilities in their community school.

As part of this adapted educational curriculum, they most often receive direct physical and occupational therapy during the school day. Often speech and language therapy services are provided as well. Additional programs in adaptive physical education complement the school day.

In the field of rehabilitation and education for the child with a brain injury, there is controversy about whether these classrooms are appropriate. Some professionals believe children with traumatic brain injuries should not be in classrooms with children who have severe mental disabilities.

These classrooms can work very appropriately if the school staff are made aware of the injury and given the opportunity to provide an educational program specifically suited to the child's needs. In fact, there are many teachers in these programs who have provided a creative, cognitively appropriate program for the child with a brain injury. These teachers are very quick to notice a child's progress and do not hesitate to recommend a less restrictive educational environment when indicated.

Programming for infants and toddlers is more difficult. It is harder to obtain such intensive services for children at younger ages. Most commonly, the child is seen in the home by a collection of professionals from the community school and rehabilitation agencies. Generally this includes an infant teacher, a speech-language pathologist, a physical therapist, and an occupational therapist. In Minnesota, children qualify for center-based programming at 3 years of age.

Children discharged to foster homes receive the same educational and therapeutic adaptations as those who go home.

Children who are placed in a residential facility receive the same educational program in the community. Often they receive additional therapies in the residence.

## The Role of the Speech-Language Pathologist

The speech-language pathologist in the acute rehabilitation center assists in the smooth transitioning of these children. This role can be summarized as follows:

- teaching the school-based speech-language pathologist the parameters of an appropriate stimulation and attention program

- assisting the family and community professionals in understanding why an augmentative communication system is not appropriate at this cognitive level

- teaching the family and professionals the techniques of an oral stimulation and/or feeding program

## Nontraditional Approaches

It is at this time in recovery—when a child has made minimal progress and the family is preparing for discharge—that many parents begin to investigate nontraditional medical approaches. These can range from chiropractic therapies to healing services. In between are programs that use intensive physical programming, diet, and acupuncture.

*At this point, the family does not need your judgment that these alternative methods are hokus pokus. I, too, would probably seek alternative methods if, in my estimation, the traditional medical model was not working. It is very important to encourage the family to maintain relationships with the rehabilitation physician and therapists to help monitor progress, regardless of what additional therapies the child receives.*

Discharging the child who is in such great need of service requires organization, planning, and solid teamwork. The family is always at the core of this process and being taught, supported, and encouraged. The energy flow to accomplish all this can be dissipated periodically by the sadness everyone feels that the child is not better.

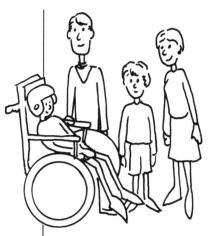

The discharge of the higher functioning child is somehow less cumbersome. But that process too becomes difficult and sad over the years. The child with a brain injury in a classroom is too often minimally programmed, undersupported educationally, and isolated emotionally.

## Discharge of the Child at Levels 2 and 1

The dictionary definition of *discharge* creates a rather negative image: unloading, dismissing, to relieve oneself of a burden or obligation. Perhaps this frame of reference is one of the reasons families feel abandoned or anxious around the issue of discharge.

It is critical, therefore, to approach discharge as a process of transition that begins upon admission. A well-organized discharge plan is one that creates **a two-way bridge** from the hospital to home, community, and school. A child who is discharged should never be dismissed from the program. There has to be ongoing exchange of information between the acute setting and the community with a continuum of care that extends until adulthood, when necessary.

The process of discharge at Levels 2 and 1 is somewhat different from the process of discharging a child who remains in a functional coma. What is the same is that discharge variables such as the age of the child, the school setting, the family dynamics, the geographical location, and the cognitive and physical condition of the child all influence the course of discharge.

For example, if there are readily available services in the child's school, discharge may take place weeks in advance of a child who is returning to a school where no services are available. A family who is able to provide a full-time caretaker is usually ready to take their child home sooner than a family where both parents work, or a single-parent family where the parent works and will have to hire help or rely on family members to care for a child in the parent's absence.

Whatever the case, the most important goal of discharge is to implement education and training to prepare the child, family, and school for transitioning from the acute setting to continued recovery and rehabilitation in the home, school, and community setting.

## Discharge of the Structure-Dependent (Level 2) Child

In earlier years, children were discharged in one of two states: those who were in a functional coma, and those who were in Level 1, oriented but not fully recovered.

However, with the decreased length of stay and the increased abilities of the schools to deal with the child who has a brain injury, children are more frequently being discharged who are still at Level 2 or not consistently at Level 1.

There are several characteristics of this group of children that are worth repeating because they significantly affect the child's safety and educational needs.

These children are still lacking the memory skills to store and retrieve information consistently. Their learning style will require redundancy, repetition, props, and the expectation that the same material may need to be repeated the next day.

There is a tremendous temptation to equip nonverbal or severely dysarthric children with a sophisticated communication device (discussed in Chapter 8). A reminder: carefully assess the child's ability to use a device prior to any recommendation for a purchase!

Constant supervision is a must. These children are impulsive, disoriented, and distractible. They will likely require a paraprofessional in school to help them find their way, remain on task, and be safe.

Stimulation overload may still be a factor, and these children may require rest periods or shortened school days.

In the home, beyond the obvious modifications for wheelchairs, bathchairs, canes, and any other adaptive devices, the parents may require a personal-care attendant for the child so that other children in the family can have their needs met. Families may benefit from respite care because the demands of the Level 2 child both physically and emotionally can place a tremendous strain on the caregivers.

Discharge testing of Level 2 children presents quite a challenge. It is important to attempt and achieve formalized testing whenever possible. This information will help school personnel and the family establish an appropriate level of interaction and education. At the same time, it must be realized that testing at this level is a gross estimation, and that observation of children in their environment also gives valuable information as to how they are perceiving, processing, and reacting.

These children are structure-dependent, and that must be kept in mind as the discharge process begins.

# Discharge of the Concrete Processor (Level 1) Child

At Level 1, the task of discharge would appear to be a much easier job. Many of these children are physically able to navigate with minimal to no assistance. They are oriented, and memory skills are improving. However, it is probably the more subtle needs that dictate that careful assessment and planning take place.

The March 1991 issue of *The Journal of Head Trauma Rehabilitation* is devoted to school re-entry following head injury. This resource contains excellent discussions of issues such as placement, transition, testing, assessment of adolescents, adapting programs, higher education, and educating the educators. It is encouraging to note the tremendous increase in information regarding the educational needs of the child with a traumatic brain injury.

## Discharge Assessment

Rather than listing here all the possible assessment tools and the age ranges for the various disciplines, this information has been included in Appendix B. Each center has their favorite tools, and new tools are constantly being developed and marketed.

When reporting standardized test performance, it is important to explain that the child's performance on testing does not guarantee that the child is able to use these skills in all environments or to generalize them to all situations. Certain skills may be elicited only in very structured, distraction-free environments.

## Beyond Assessment

An excellent article in the *Journal of Learning Disabilities* describes many of the difficulties faced by hospital personnel and the schools in making appropriate placement plans for the child with a traumatic brain injury. Studies indicate that children placed in regular classroom settings based solely on their intellectual functioning experience increasing failure one and two years following their injuries (Telzrow 1987).

The frustration of dealing with a child with a "normal" IQ but significant residual deficits following traumatic brain injury is aptly described in the following letter sent in prior to a young boy's clinic visit:

> A. has poor organizational skills. He seldom remembers to bring necessary materials to class and, even when reminded to get ready for his reading group, usually has to go back to his room to hunt for something. His work has seldom been completed on time.
>
> He daydreams, sometimes puts his books away, and just sits at his empty desk until I remind him to get back to work. A. seems to have a short attention span and cannot sit still for very long.

He fiddles and plays often with pencils, rubber bands, and so forth.

He also tends to hum or whistle at inappropriate times even after being asked not to. He has difficulty completing assignments by himself. My main concern about A. is his lack of a sense of responsibility for himself.

There are additional observations that must be included in a comprehensive assessment to provide the school with a more complete description of the child's performance.

In their article, *School re-entry following head injury: Managing the transition from hospital to school,* Ylvisaker, Hartwick, and Stevens (1991) stress the need to explore the child's ability to learn and adapt in a classroom-like environment with the following variables:

- environmental factors—including noise levels, activity levels, consistency in staff

- schedule—including length of session, consistency in schedule, free versus scheduled time, time of day (endurance)

- cuing systems—including assignment book, task cues (such as advance organizers), repeated instructions, written instructions, buddy system (for getting from class to class or for remembering assignments), maps for navigation within the school

- modification in materials/tests—including enlarged print, simplified worksheets, take-home tests, extra time

- instructional variables—including task analysis, best sensory modality, compensatory strategies, self-paced instructional plans, competency-based instruction, precision teaching, computer-assisted instruction

- classroom aids—including calculator, tape recorder, writing aids, positioning equipment, augmentative communication device, environmental control equipment

- work expectations—including quality of work, length of assignments, independent work, rate of performance

- motivational variables—including reinforcers, schedule of reinforcement, need for success/reaction to failure, need for immediate reward

Ideally, this process is begun well in advance of discharge. School personnel should be included in sessions to observe, to provide input, and to carry information back to other school personnel.

Videotaping a child in the acute setting is frequently a valuable tool for the school, particularly if distance prevents frequent visits or any visits at all.

Whenever possible, key staff members accompany a videotape to the school. It often reassures the school staff to have these key professionals present to introduce the tape and to be available to answer questions or prevent misinterpretations or misunderstandings. The child and family may or may not decide to be in the classroom for "the premiere."

In providing recommendations to the school, it is critical to solicit the school's input as part of the process. It is tempting to expect the same level of services in the school as the child has been receiving in the hospital. However, this is rarely possible. Schools are not staffed to offer medically-based therapy.

The purpose of occupational therapy, physical therapy, and speech and language services in the school is to help the child achieve instructional or educational goals. This may include, for example, asking the occupational therapist to assist in adapting a writing device to enable the student to complete worksheets, or to instruct the child in the use of a computer for word-processing skills if the child is no longer able to write in an efficient manner.

If the child is in need of therapy services that exceed the school's capabilities, it may be necessary to provide outpatient services in addition to the child's school day. It is possible, in some cases, to work with the school to provide therapy following a half day at school.

The Minnesota Head Injury Association has recently published a very readable guide for parents entitled, *I'm a parent of a child with a head/brain injury. How can I work with the school?* (Mencel 1991; available by calling 1-800-669-MHIA). In a step-by-step fashion, it outlines questions parents should ask and appropriate ways to interact with the school system in order to obtain the necessary programs and services for the child.

Enlisting the support of a parent advocacy group is often helpful in obtaining support and information. In Minnesota, the PACER Center (Parent Advocacy Coalition for Educational Rights) is an extremely well-organized and highly visible resource for parents and schools. Further information can be obtained by calling 1-800-53PACER.

## Legislation and the Child with a Brain Injury

Recent changes in legislation should make it easier for children and their families to obtain an appropriate educational setting.

The Education of the Handicapped Act has been renamed to Individuals with Disabilities Education Act (IDEA) or P.L. 101-476. Eligibility for special education services now includes children with traumatic brain injury. "IDEA expressly lists therapeutic recreation, social work services, and rehabilitation counseling as examples of related services that a school may be required to provide" (Savage 1992).

Continued follow-up is a must. A well-organized pediatric rehabilitation program provides outpatient clinics to assess the child's ongoing physical, cognitive, and social needs and to offer suggestions as requested by family and school. Even though children may seem to be progressing nicely as they return to kindergarten, first, and second grade, these same children present high risk for academic difficulties as the demands for increased abstract thinking and independent functioning increase.

The transition from elementary to middle school may require many adjustments in their programs. The same may be true at the high school level.

IDEA now requires transition planning and services. "Beginning no later than age 16 (and, in some cases, age 14 or younger), Individual Education Plans must include a statement of the transition services the student will need before leaving the school" (Savage 1992).

These services are to include any instruction that will assist in post-secondary education, vocational training, integrated employment, continuing and adult education, adult services, independent living, and community integration.

There is a tremendous need for supported living situations which allow young adults to live as independently as possible in a safe environment. It is now mandated that the IEP will include instruction in acquisition of daily living skills and will work with other agencies to transition the young adult to independent living.

● ● ● ● ●

Throughout this discussion it has been stressed that *discharge* should not imply *termination*. Discharge is transition. And due to the interruption in the natural course of development, traumatic brain injury results in the need to transition the child through most major steps from the time of injury through adulthood. A closer look at outcome for these children is discussed in the following chapter on current research.

# Current Research

It is not the purpose of this chapter to cover all research pertinent to pediatric brain injury. Rather, the following topics will be considered:

- incidence and cause of brain injury

- type of injury and outcome

- age of injury and outcome

- studies of educational outcome

## Incidence and Cause of Brain Injury

It has been estimated that more than one million children sustain traumatic head injuries each year in the United States. For children and adolescents, accidents are the leading cause of both death and disability, with brain injuries predominating. With advances in medical science, the mortality rate for disease that previously accounted for most childhood deaths has decreased. This has resulted in increased focus on the importance of injuries in childhood.

In the United States, approximately 200 of every 100,000 children sustain traumatic brain injuries each year and approximately 10 of every 100,000 children between birth and 14 years of age die from these injuries (Kraus, Fife, and Cox 1986). The mortality from brain injury is decreasing as the management of children in trauma centers and emergency rooms has improved. As a result, the need for comprehensive rehabilitation settings continues to rise.

Causes of brain injuries in children vary with the age of the child and are closely linked to developmental capabilities. Falls are more common in infancy and toddler years; pedestrian accidents predominate in preschool and early school years; and driver and passenger injuries (often related to alcohol and drug use) and sports injuries rank the highest during adolescence. However, throughout all age groups, automobile-related accidents are a major cause of severe and fatal injuries.

In infancy, most traumatic brain injuries are secondary to falls or child abuse. Very young infants are at risk when placed on surfaces such as infant changing tables, furniture, or counters. During infancy and the toddler years there is a high incidence of brain injury because young children are unable to protect themselves from harm caused by their own exploration or by other people.

As described in Chapter 1, young children are also vulnerable because of their cranial anatomy. Sadly, the outcome for injured infants who are severely abused may be significantly worse than those who are injured in accidents (Brink, Imbus, and Woo-Sam 1980).

Young children can also receive brain injuries as passengers in automobiles, especially if they are not properly restrained.

The preschool years continue to present high risk for traumatic brain injuries. The primary cause continues to be falls, but an increasing number of children are injured as pedestrians hit by cars. This is understandable because children at this age are expanding their world to include the neighborhood.

At this time behavioral characteristics may begin to influence the child's risk for injury. Hyperactivity, attention deficits, and decreased compliance may contribute to a greater risk of injury (Klonhoff 1971).

The school-age years produce the fewest brain injuries when compared to rates in infancy, the toddler years, and adolescence. Motor vehicle accidents continue to account for the highest number, with children either as passengers or pedestrians. Sports-related injuries increase during this period, with many accidents involving bicycles, skateboards, and baseball bats (Klonhoff 1971).

As expected, the incidence of brain injuries, which remains relatively stable throughout childhood, increases dramatically in the teenage years. The number of severe injuries in the 15- to 19-year-old range equals that of all the previous 14 years combined (Gross et al. 1985).

Whether some children are more likely than others to sustain injury is an area of conflicting research. There is relative agreement as to which behaviors are more likely to be related to injury: impulsivity, inattention, emotional lability, risk taking, competitiveness, and aggressiveness.

A prospective study in Britain (Butler and Golding 1986) clarifies accident variables in children 5 years and younger. This report is important because it involves a comprehensive follow-up of children born during one week, April 5 to April 11, 1970. Of the approximately 16,000 children studied after birth, 17 had died from accidents or violence by the age of 5. Of these 17 deaths, 12 were related to brain injuries: 7 motor vehicle accidents, 2 objects falling on children, and 3 nonaccidental injuries.

As in the Annegers study (1983), the Butler and Golding study showed that boys not only had more accidents than girls but were also likely to have repeated accidents. Children with more than one accident showed differences in behavior. They were more likely to be described as disobedient, destructive, hyperactive, and fighting with other children. Their mothers were likely to be young, employed, heavy smokers, and living in urban areas.

Additional research and more complete information is needed on the various etiologies of brain injury. This work needs to be focused on preventing injuries as well as treating them. Workable strategies need to be developed for reducing disability and death and the emotional and financial expense to children, their families, and society.

# Types of Injuries and Outcomes

## Anoxic Injuries

Drowning is the fourth most common cause of accidental death in childhood, and in children younger than 5 years of age, it is the third leading cause of accidental death (Shephard 1989).

The single most important step in the treatment of submersion accidents is the immediate institution of resuscitative measures. For the apneic victim, that means mouth-to-mouth resuscitation must begin as soon as the rescuer reaches the victim. Oxygen at the highest concentration attainable should be provided to the victim as soon as possible.

The most significant and important complication of near-drowning accidents, in addition to pulmonary injury, is the anoxic-ischemic cerebral insult. Most of the late deaths and long-term results of near-drowning stem from brain insults.

Various scoring systems have been developed to predict which pediatric patients will do well after a near-drowning accident. Orlowski (1987) delineated five unfavorable prognostic factors:

- age less than 3 years

- estimated maximum submersion time longer than five minutes

- no attempts at resuscitation for at least ten minutes after the rescue

- patient in coma on admission to emergency room

- arterial blood gas Ph less than 7.10

Patients with two or fewer poor prognostic factors had a 90% chance of good recovery with standard treatment, whereas patients with three or more prognostic factors had only a 5% chance of good recovery.

Recent data suggest that patients who remain in a deep coma for two to six hours after the submersion will do poorly—they will either be brain dead or suffer moderate to severe neurological impairment. Patients who are improving but remain unresponsive have a 50/50 chance of doing well. Patients who are definitely improving and are alert or are stuporous but respond to stimuli two to six hours after the accident will generally do well, and most will have normal or near-normal neurological outcomes.

A group of near-drowning victims that has received a great deal of publicity are those who have been submersed in very cold or ice water. In 17 cases of children who experienced prolonged submersion with good outcomes, all incidents occurred in water 10° C or less (Orlowski 1987). In these cases, hypothermia (reduced body temperature) induced by exposure to the very cold water or ice is thought to protect the brain and other organs from anoxia.

One study examined the survival and outcome of 36 children with tracheostomies and gastrostomies. The children had experienced anoxic metabolic encephalopathies (AME) or traumatic head injuries (TI) (Splaingar et al. 1989). AME included near drowning, cardiac arrest, attempted hanging, shock, and diabetic encephalopathy.

Of the 22 children with severe traumatic injury, ten achieved independence in three functional areas (locomotion, self-care, and communication) by two years, whereas none of the 14 with AME achieved functional independence in any area at two years.

Two points must be made in regard to this study. These were severe injuries as indicated by the children's requirements for tracheostomies and gastrostomies. Secondly, as a group, children with severe anoxic insults recover less well than children with severe traumatic brain injuries.

## Minor Head Injury

A growing number of authors have examined the sequelae of minor head injury.

Case studies reported by Fuld and Fisher (1977) indicated that children with normal EEGs and neurological examinations continued to show serious post-traumatic intellectual impairments long past the point where they had been diagnosed as "back to normal" by their physicians.

A major study of neurobehavioral sequelae of minor head injuries in children was undertaken by the departments of pediatrics and neurology at The Johns Hopkins University School of Medicine, and the department of pediatrics at Sinai Hospital, Baltimore (Farmer et al. 1987). Behavioral symptoms in 247 children with mild head injuries were compared to those in 280 children with trauma to other regions of the body.

For this study, minor head trauma was defined as "no alteration of consciousness lasting for more than several seconds, there was no prolonged memory loss in children where this was testable, and neurological examination was normal on initial evaluation."

This study indicates that children with very mild head injuries are likely to experience symptoms similar to those experienced by children with body trauma: behavioral problems (such as clinging, irritability, sleep disturbance, and hyperactivity) and transient headaches for the mild head trauma patients. While short-lived, these behaviors can be interfering to a child returning to school.

Indeed, researchers working with adolescents who have had mild closed head injuries found that teens require more follow-up services to return successfully to school (Jacobson et al. 1986). They suggest that this need is due to the developmental stages in adolescence that are naturally problematic and become increasingly so in the presence of mild brain injury.

# Other Factors Affecting Outcome

## Age at Injury

Contrary to many of the early studies of pediatric brain injury, contemporary studies are looking more closely at the very young brain and concluding that trauma at this age has a much more profound effect on development than earlier studies indicated.

As described in Chapter 1, the young brain is of a softer consistency, with less protection from its bony covering. Infants younger than 5 months of age have been found to suffer a very characteristic and typical brain injury consisting of gross tears in the subcortical white matter of the temporal and orbitofrontal lobes (Raimondi and Hirschauer 1989).

In examining the outcomes of 1- to 3-year-old children with closed-head injuries, Raimondi and Hirschauer (1989) found that children of 1 year and younger were likely to have a poorer outcome.

Similarly, children younger than 2 years of age had a worse outcome as compared to older children in a long-term study of children with severe head trauma (Mahoney et al. 1983) It was suggested that the poorer outcome of the infants may be due to the greater shearing forces in the less-myelinated immature brain, or to the young brain's reduced ability to deal with rapid swelling.

A very interesting study of outcome related to age followed 97 children in a traumatic brain injury unit in a pediatric hospital (Kriel, Krach, and Panser 1989). Patients were divided into two categories: those injured before and those injured after the age of 6. Children 6 years or older had better cognitive and motor outcomes than those injured before 6 years of age.

The differences between the two groups were thought to be etiological. Some of the children in the under-6 group received brain injuries secondary to abuse. It was suspected that these children had had previous abuse injuries resulting in the poorer outcomes for the current injuries. When abused children were removed from the study, outcomes were similar.

A brain injury, regardless of when it occurs, interrupts the ability to learn and, most specifically, to learn new information.

## Length of Coma

In study after study, length of coma has been found to be a reasonable predictor for functional outcome.

An enlightening study regarding prognostic implications for children in persistent vegetative states measured outcome following prolonged un-consciousness (Kriel, Krach, and Sheehan 1988). Children with traumatic brain injuries who had been in coma longer than 90 days were studied.

Functional outcome of the group was correlated with degree of cerebral atrophy as demonstrated by computerized (CT) scan. Of the 26 children in the group, 20 were unconscious for 12 to 45 weeks and six remained in a persistent vegetative state.

For this study, consciousness was defined as the ability to follow commands or gestured requests, respond socially, discriminate animate versus inanimate objects, and spontaneously initiate adaptive behavior.

The children were followed at six-month intervals for two years. While these children experienced far from what would be considered a functional recovery, they continued to get better after discharge. Four of the children tested with an IQ of greater than 70, and all of those children were older than 12 at the time of injury. Seven were considered functional communicators, able to make their needs known verbally; nine were socially responsive; and six remained in persistent vegetative state. One child died secondary to an episode of status epilepticus.

There was great variability in the motor outcomes: four children walked independently, one walked with a walker, four required adult assistance for ambulation, ten were nonambulatory, and seven showed no purpose-ful movement.

This study is one of very few measuring long-term outcome of children in coma longer than 90 days. While six remained in a persistent vegetative state and one died, 19 regained consciousness, most of those with some cognitive and motor reacquisition.

A study conducted by Stover and Zeiger (1976) indicates that patients in coma over seven days did not make a complete recovery to pre-injury personality or psychological or physical status. Those children in coma less than 13 weeks, with the exception of one, were able to regain the ability to walk. Of the ten patients who came out of coma after 13 weeks, only two achieved independent ambulation.

These findings are very similar to outcome data collected in a pilot study by Kriel, Krach, and Sheehan (1984). Outcome following traumatic brain injury was best predicted by length of coma.

All children who remained in coma from five to 12 weeks required some type of specialized services upon return to school. Approximately one-third of this group regained the ability to walk independently, one-third required assistance to walk, and one-third required a wheelchair as their primary means of mobility. The majority of children in this five- to 12-week group had some residual dysarthria or slurring of speech.

Children in coma from one to four weeks have a better prognosis when it comes to walking and speech. However, most of these children also require special services to help them return successfully to their school settings.

Children who regained consciousness in less than a week recovered speech, walking, and self-care skills. Most of these children also demonstrated IQ scores within the normal range. However, the more subtle difficulties with cognitive skills frequently interfered with school performance.

A direct correlation between the duration of coma and the measured intelligence after injury was documented in a study of 52 children in coma longer than one week (Brink et al. 1970). They documented increased intellectual deficits in the younger age group as compared to the adolescent group. They, too, raise concern regarding academic performance for all children following traumatic brain injury.

# Educational Outcome

Much has been written in recent years regarding education of the child with traumatic brain injury and transitioning from the acute rehabilitation setting to the school setting. The March 1991 issue of *The Journal of Head Trauma Rehabilitation* focuses on issues related to school re-entry following head injury.

It is through the efforts of professionals such as Sally Cohen, Ron Savage, Mark Ylvisaker, Cathy Telzrow, Ellen Lehr, and numerous others that the medical and educational communities have become increasingly aware of the special needs of the child with TBI. As one of our colleagues aptly stated "These children can learn to read, but they can't read to learn."

In an excellent article, Telzrow (1987) describes many of the difficulties faced by hospital personnel and the schools in making appropriate placement plans. The article cites studies indicating that children placed in regular classroom settings experience increasing failure one and two years following their injuries.

A study that followed a group of 231 children up to five years post-injury found that 15% of the younger group and nearly 18% of the older students experienced successive school failure or withdrew from school (Klonhoff, Low, and Clark 1977).

In one pilot study, nearly half of the children in coma less than a week required some type of special school services upon return to school (Kriel, Krach, and Sheehan 1984). In fact, 60% of the children in coma from one to four weeks required special services for up to six months following injury. Children in coma five to 12 weeks were rarely able to return to the mainstream of school.

Standard IQ tests are not always sensitive to the subtle cognitive sequelae of even more severe brain injuries. Nevertheless, these deficits continue to plague children in all facets of their lives.

● ● ● ● ●

It is critical for professionals working in the area of traumatic brain injury and education to continue to advocate for the needs of the children and their families. Research efforts examining outcome of acute care, long-term outcome, and educational programming need to continue to provide the best services possible.

# Out of Harm's Way: Prevention of Injury

● ● ● ● ●

One of the most difficult issues we deal with on a daily basis is our own personal feelings of vulnerability, and how we reconcile these tragedies within our families and circle of friends. The critical issue, of course, is balancing our own feelings of vulnerability without making our families and friends totally paranoid about getting in an accident.

It is pretty scary to be confronted on a *daily basis* with the reality that children get hurt—an apparently randomly occurring tragedy can suddenly interrupt a child's life and wrap a family in hurt and fear forever.

The flip side of this vocational coin—marked vulnerability—is gratitude for health, but we both admit to a fear and trepidation about our own children's precarious wellness. This is especially true because these children of ours climb, run, jump, swim, learn to drive, play sports, and are basically childhood verbs, as described earlier. We would like to—*but they would never let us*—send them off to their various activities encased in a plastic bubble!

I remember going to pick up my daughter at horse camp when she was 9. As I drove up and gazed over the green meadow and the youthful group of horse-loving 9-year-olds, it was certainly easy to spot which one had a mother who worked on a brain injury unit for children—she was the only camper in a protective helmet!

Perhaps, in some respects, this chapter is more important than others in this book because we really don't want these injuries to happen in the first place. It would be better if it hadn't had to be written or read.

This chapter will discuss the concept of the word *accident,* summarize incidence figures, outline ways to prevent and/or reduce injuries, and describe the cost of these injuries financially.

● ● ● ● ●

# Accident?

The word *accidental* is defined in the American Heritage Dictionary as "occurring unexpectedly and unintentionally; by chance." Generally the word *accident* in this society is used to describe a randomly occurring event. But when one looks more closely, it is sometimes questionable whether the event was totally random.

There are children who end up in brain-injury programs who have a history of previous visits to the emergency room with broken bones, scrapes, and cuts; children who walk the wild side by playing "chicken" with motorized vehicles or playing with guns; children who climb cliffs; and children who sled into busy streets.

There are children who are unsupervised most of their day, children whose parents have guns in the home, and children who live in families without a high value placed on personal safety or health. When these children get hurt, are the events as random as intimated? Are they not "in harm's way"?

Clearly, there are many children whose injuries were the result of a random occurrence. For example, a child's horse can unexpectedly kick that child in the head. Children can be walking along a sidewalk when a car goes out of control and comes up on the pavement to hit the child. Children who are properly restrained ride in cars that are hit by drivers who run red lights or ignore stop signs. Children who are safely crossing streets are struck by drunk drivers.

But there are also children who seem, by way of history, to be more at risk. The term *accident* needs to be more carefully defined in the incidence of brain injury. Prevention programs should perhaps concentrate on these high-risk groups.

## Indices of Child Health in the National Context

Members of the League of Women Voters in Minnesota voted at their 1985 convention to study children's health issues. They conducted interviews with more than 70 professionals and advocates concerned with child health services, and the report was published in 1987. It begins with these haunting goals:

- Goal 1: All children should be wanted and born well to healthy mothers.

- Goal 2: All children should receive adequate and appropriate preventative health care which includes the prevention of death and disease and the promotion of physical, intellectual, social, and emotional health.

- Goal 3: All adolescents and youth should live in a social setting that recognizes their special health, personal, and social needs.

- Goal 4: All children with chronic handicaps should be able to function at their optimal level.

- Goal 5: All children should live in an environment that is as free as possible from hazards to their health and development.

- Goal 6: All children should be educated about health and health care systems.

These goals are haunting in the context of the current health care system because the problems inherent in this Darwinian system have grave implications for its most vulnerable members.

> Children are known to be resilient and adaptable. Children are also known to be vulnerable and easily damaged by social, psychic, and physical traumas and neglect. If children are blighted by failures to meet their need, what are the long- and short-term costs to society? (Miller, Fine, and Adams-Taylor 1989, 2)

How do this nation's health policies and resources fit its smallest citizens? Health policy "may be regarded as the aggregate of principles or themes that prevail in the ways society distributes its resources and power as they relate to the determinants of a population's state of health" (Miller, Fine, and Adams-Taylor 1989, 2).

"Resources" refers to goods, money, and power as they relate to health care. The benefactors are determined among competing interest groups such as the medical profession, hospitals, insurance companies, health industry entrepreneurs, government, and large employers.

Considerations of the biological and medical determinants of health have usually dominated health policy, which has generally produced advances in biomedical technology.

Problems about access to this ever-increasing technology have not been resolved. It seems that state-of-the-art medical care is rationed over who can pay for it. In matters of health policy, medical answers are sought to social problems. This approach is done at great expense, but it seems that this is preferable to developing social reforms that might have a more meaningful impact on health status.

The cost of giving one child all recommended child health preventive services from birth to age 20 is approximately equal to the cost of one day in the hospital. Unfortunately, too often children's health needs are addressed only when they are acutely ill. (Giebink 1986)

Miller, Fine, and Adams-Taylor (1989) attempted to strengthen the foundation of solid data on which sound policy in matters of children's health can be built. Twelve indicators of children's health were fully described, data sources identified, and policy implications reviewed. These indicators are representative of child health problems that can be prevented or reduced.

Of those parameters, three that influence children with brain injuries will be discussed in this chapter: (1) non-motor-vehicle accident fatalities, (2) motor vehicle accident fatalities, and (3) child abuse and neglect.

## Non-Motor-Vehicle Accident Fatalities

### Definition

An accident or injury fatality is a death that results from an unanticipated and unintended event. Drowning, fires, burns, and falls are among the leading causes of accidental death for children and youth. Other major causes of non-motor-vehicle accident fatalities include aspiration of food and objects, poisoning by solids or liquids, and poisoning by gas.

### Indicator

Indicators are defined as the rate of non-motor-vehicle accident fatalities (deaths per 100,000) for the following age groups: under 1, 1 to 4, 5 to 9, 10 to 14, and 15 to 19.

### Significance

The road to adulthood is filled with natural and unnatural hazards.

- Vulnerable infants cannot perceive dangers in their environment, and even if they do primitively perceive danger, they cannot move out of harm's way.

- Toddlers have a predisposition to physical injury because of their natural curiosity, unbalanced by wisdom or experience.

- School-age children are carefree and careless. Both qualities are essential for a happy and explorative childhood, but these characteristics are sometimes incompatible with life.

- Teenagers are known to be risk takers, a factor that seems to be inherent in their struggle to grow up. However, some of these risks land the teenager in the hospital or morgue.

Nonfatal injuries account for half of all visits to hospital and emergency rooms (Barancik et al. 1983). Millions of children are injured seriously enough each year to require some kind of medical treatment.

Children who survive accidental injuries may suffer permanent physical or mental damage requiring extensive treatment or extended care for a chronic condition. Possible consequences to survivors include brain damage, broken bones, spinal cord injuries, internal organ injuries, extensive scarring, loss of limbs, and loss of vision or hearing.

The rate of death from non-motor-vehicle accidents reflects the extent to which a society effectively regulates the safety of consumer products, implements and enforces codes to ensure safe and adequate housing, provides adequate child care for working parents, maintains safe public spaces, provides poison control hotlines, ensures access to services and emergency medical care when an injury does occur, promotes the use of child-proof packaging for potential poisons, and educates the public regarding accident prevention (Miller, Fine, and Adams-Taylor 1989).

## Status and Trends

In 1985, non-motor-vehicle accidents accounted for 40% of all accidental deaths during childhood. More than 6,400 U.S. children and youths under age 20 died as a result of injury in non-motor-vehicle accidents.

Overall, the lowest rates of death are among children ages 5 to 9. In 1985, the rate of non-motor-vehicle accident fatalities for this age group was 5.5 per 100,000. The rates for other age groups were as follows: infants under age 1, 19.0; preschoolers from 1 to 4 years, 12.9; adolescents from 10 to 14 years, 5.9; and teens from 15 to 19 years, 10.3 (National Center for Health Statistics 1987).

## Risk Factors

At greatest risk of non-motor-vehicle accidental injury are children and youths from low-income and poorly educated families, those who live in inadequate or deteriorating housing, and those living under unusually stressful conditions. There is also some evidence that children with history of injury are at increased risk of subsequent accidental injury (Feldman 1980). Generally, boys are at greater risk than girls for accidental injury across all age groups. This is often explained as reflecting boys' increased interest in risk-taking.

## U.S. Objective

The U.S. Department of Health and Human Services (1980) set the following objective for reducing the rate of home accident fatalities among children:

> By 1990 the rate of home accident fatalities for children under age 15 should be no greater than 5.0 per 100,000 children.

Home accident fatalities are a subset of non-motor-vehicle accident fatalities. Objectives for reducing fatalities from falls, drowning, and fires and burns are for the population as a whole, not specifically for children.

### Progress

It was difficult to find progress statistics for this category because of the many subsets and differing age groupings when reported. However, figures from *Accident facts* (1987), a publication of the National Safety Council, reported non-motor-vehicle accident fatalities in 1986 as follows: under age 1, 19.86; ages 1 to 4, 13.2; and ages 5 to 14, 5.6. These figures are slightly higher than 1985 in all age groups. This is a long way from the goal of 5.0 for 100,000 children.

## Motor Vehicle Accident Fatalities

### Definition

A motor vehicle accident fatality is a death resulting from a motor vehicle accident, whether the victim is a passenger, pedestrian, cyclist, or driver.

### Indicator

Indicators are defined as the rate of motor vehicle accident fatalities (deaths per 100,000 population) for the following age groups: under 1, 1 to 4, 5 to 14, and 15 to 19.

### Significance

As a nation, great strides have generally been made in preventing or reducing childhood deaths from various diseases. However, similar progress has not occurred in reducing the rate of motor vehicle accident fatalities during childhood and adolescence. Although legislative, regulatory, educational, and other initiatives have met with some success, motor vehicle accidents remain a major cause of premature and largely preventable death.

The rate of motor vehicle fatalities is a measure of the adequacy or inadequacy of a broad range of public health interventions, including:

- implementation and enforcement of programs and policies requiring or facilitating use of safety restraints for auto passengers and helmets for cyclists

- improving the safety design of vehicles and highways

- lowering the maximum speed limit

- developing alternative bike paths

- raising the legal age for drinking or driving or both

- imposing more stringent penalties on drunk drivers

- taking other measures that reduce the incidence of driving under the influence of alcohol

## Status and Trends

Accidents are the leading cause of death among persons from 1 to 19 years of age. In 1985, more than eight out of ten deaths in the age group were due to accidents, and motor vehicle accidents specifically accounted for 56% of the deaths in this age group.

Sporadic declines in the rate of motor vehicle deaths among teens have occurred in the past two decades. Nonetheless, in 1985, more than 40% of all deaths among 15- to 19-year-olds were the result of motor vehicle accidents, producing a death rate of 33.9 per 100,000, more than three times the 10.0 rate for suicide, the second leading cause of death for this age group (Miller, Fine, and Adams-Taylor 1989).

Death rates for various kinds of motor vehicle accidents show distinctive patterns by age: the peak death rates for pedestrians are at ages 5 and 18; for bicyclists, ages 11 to 15; for automobile occupants, ages 18 to 20; and for motorcyclists, ages 18 to 22 (Baker, O'Neil, and Karpf 1984).

Males continue to outnumber females as victims of fatal motor vehicle accidents, with the disparity increasing in each childhood age group. In 1985, the rate of motor vehicle accident fatalities for male infants was about the same as that for female infants, but the rate for males was 2.3 times the rate for females among 15- to 19-year-olds.

Miller, Fine, and Adams-Taylor (1989) also report that restrained children are 50% to 70% less likely to be injured in an auto accident than unrestrained children. The rate of restraint usage for children younger than 5 years rose from 6% in 1980 to 28% in 1986. Additionally, children who survived an auto accident were more likely to have been restrained than those who died (45% versus 26%). The National Health Interview Survey reports that only one-third of children under age 7 use seat belts regularly.

All 50 states and the District of Columbia have implemented laws requiring use of restraints for young children in automobiles. As a result of such laws, Michigan witnessed a 25% decrease in the number of children under age 4 injured in crashes, and New Mexico experienced a 33% reduction in fatality rates and a 13% reduction in injuries to children younger than age 5 (Miller, Fine, and Adams-Taylor 1989).

Alcohol is a contributing factor in approximately 20% of all crashes resulting in an injury, 50% of all fatal crashes, and 60% of all fatal crashes involving a single vehicle. In 1985, 3,860 children under age 20 died in alcohol-related motor vehicle accidents (Miller, Fine, and Adams-Taylor 1989).

### Risk Factors

Among children and youths, adolescent males are at greatest risk for dying in a motor vehicle accident. Experimentation with alcohol, combined with driving inexperience, increases the teenager's risk of being involved in fatal motor vehicle accidents (Center for Disease Control 1982).

### U.S. Objectives for Reducing Motor Vehicle Fatalities

In 1980, the U.S. Department of Health and Human Services set the following objective for reducing motor vehicle fatalities among children and youths:

By 1990, the rate of motor vehicle fatalities for children under age 15 should be reduced to no greater than 5.5 per 100,000 population.

### Progress

The 1986 fatality rates have remained very similar to those reported in 1985. In the age category under 1 year, the rate was 4.9; the rate for 1 to 4 years was 7.0; and in the 5- to 15-year-old category, the rate was 6.9. Once again, these figures do not reflect progress toward the objective.

## Child Abuse and Neglect

### Definition

"The term child abuse and neglect does not encompass one problem, or even two, but a multitude of problems that can occur in the day-to-day interactions between children and adults responsible for their care" (Miller, Fine, and Adams-Taylor 1989, 144).

Based on the definition used by the National Center on Child Abuse and Neglect (NCCAN), a case of child abuse or neglect is one in which, through intentional acts, a parent, guardian, or other adult caretaker causes foreseeable and avoidable injury or impairment to a child under age 18 years or contributes to the unreasonable prolongation or worsening of an existing injury or impairment in a child under age 18 years.

### Indicators

Indicators are defined as (1) the number of deaths from child abuse or neglect within a defined population, and (2) the number of confirmed cases of child abuse or neglect reported by an established surveillance team or project for a specific geographic area.

### Significance

Child abuse or neglect may result in severe and permanent physical disfigurement, disability, or death caused by burns, lacerations, fractures, contusions, hemorrhages, venereal disease, malnourishment, or untreated injury or disease.

Children who survive physical assaults or neglect may suffer profound psychosocial disturbances. Although results are not yet conclusive, the impact of child abuse and neglect is far-reaching. It is becoming apparent that maltreated children may be at increased risk of becoming delinquents or runaways, of exhibiting learning disabilities or behavioral problems, of becoming criminals as adults, and of mistreating their own children (Vachss 1982).

Deaths from and confirmed cases of child abuse and neglect represent breakdowns in the ability of family units to protect, nurture, and support children. These adverse outcomes indicate the need for a wide range of well-coordinated preventive measures that reduce the risk from specific individual, family, and social conditions associated with maltreatment.

These preventive measures could include perinatal support and parent education programs to prepare prospective parents for the task ahead, self-help support groups for abusing and neglecting parents, and family support services including crisis intervention, respite care, improvement in low-income housing, and access to job training (Miller, Fine, and Adams-Taylor 1989).

### Status and Trends

An estimated 1,000 children in the United States die from abuse or neglect each year. The number of reported cases of child abuse and neglect has increased 180% in the United States over the past nine years. In 1976, the first year that reports were available, 669,000 children were reported as maltreated. In 1985, the number of children reported as abused or neglected reached nearly 1.9 million (Miller, Fine, and Adams-Taylor 1989).

Physical abuse is the type of maltreatment most commonly linked to fatality; however, the majority of reports indicated that neglect is the most common form of maltreatment. The types of maltreatment reported vary by age and sex (Miller, Fine, and Adams-Taylor 1989). In 1985, the average age of involved children was 7.1 years.

In general, neglect is most common among young children and appears to occur less often among older children, whereas sexual and emotional maltreatment occur least often among young children and become more common as children age.

Most studies find no significant differences between the proportion of males and females reported as abused and neglected. However, girls are more likely to be abused and boys are more likely to be neglected, with the gender difference becoming more pronounced with increasing age.

### Risk Factors

Certain characteristics of the family unit and the socioeconomic environment present increased risk for abuse or neglect. Risk factors characteristic of abused or neglected children include being born prematurely, having low birth weight, or having serious defects, disabilities, or chronic illness.

Family unit factors include alcoholic parent(s), absence of either the natural mother or the natural father from the home, an unusually high level of stress in the family, violence between parents, a parent with a history of being abused as a child, and a parent who is extremely immature with unrealistically high expectations of the child.

### U.S. Objectives for Reducing Child Abuse and Neglect

The U.S. Department of Health and Human Services set the following objective for reducing maltreatment of children:

> By 1990, injuries and deaths to children inflicted by abusing parents should be reduced by at least 25%.

At the time the objective was set, reliable baseline data were unavailable. Estimates varied from 200,000 to 4 million cases occurring each year in this country. Action to prevent and reduce child abuse has been hampered by the lack of recent, reliable national data on the incidence and prevalence of the problem. Progress toward meeting objectives is thus difficult to establish.

### Progress

It was estimated in the Study of National Incidence and Prevalence of Child Abuse and Neglect (U.S. Department of Health and Human Services 1980) that more than one million children nationwide (1,025,900) met the stringent requirement of having already experienced demonstrable harm as a result of abuse and neglect. This translates into an annual incidence rate of 16.3 children per 100,000.

When children are included who had been endangered but not yet demonstrably harmed, the figure skyrockets to 25.2 children per 100,000.

## Child Health Policy: Politics and Priorities

The evidence confirms that recent trends for the health of the child in this society are unfavorable. Participation in prenatal care, rates of low birth weight, and infant mortality rates have all slowed or worsened, especially for vulnerable population subgroups.

Well-documented child abuse and neglect continue to increase. Fatalities and injuries from motor vehicle accidents have increased, associated with an increase in recreational driving, often in combination with substance abuse. Trends for non-motor-vehicle accident fatalities present no more heartening trends. One of the few indicators to improve is the rate of iron deficiency anemia among poor children, a result of widespread fortification of foods, including infant formulas (Miller, Fine, and Adams-Taylor 1989).

Unfortunately, health policy in this country does not frequently derive from data. Policy formulations that protect a presumed right to health care are not currently conspicuous in the political mainstream. Extension of the principle of social insurance to include all children fights a tough battle against other spending priorities. The advocates for improved services for children have chosen the path of pushing Medicaid eligibilities up the income scale. This course has been chosen because it seems politically feasible.

The most troublesome obstacle in the way of progress toward an enlightened health policy for children is the national debt. Even as popular sentiment grows that new initiatives are needed, the capacity to finance them is seriously constrained by an annual deficit of $150 billion.

Breaking this pattern of decreased social spending can be done only with increased taxation. This will meet with opposition, but the health, vigor, and potential for productivity of our young people certainly must take priority.

Perhaps it is too much to hope that this nation would adopt a perspective that relies on diplomatic and economic means to maintain international harmony rather than expensive military means. But in the context of our shameful infant mortality rate and the increasing rates of abuse and neglect, can we sit quietly and watch our youngest children die of preventable accidents and disease while our older children may die in war?

# Proven Ways to Prevent or Reduce Injury

The following is a summary of suggestions to help you protect yourself, your family, and friends from injury. These will not come as a surprise to anyone, but it may be helpful to be reminded.

### Occupant Restraints

The majority of states have enacted mandatory seat belt laws and have had child restraint legislation for some time. Many cars have automatic seat belts, and some now come equipped with airbags which rapidly inflate on rapid deceleration. Most cars also have back passenger seat belts and even shoulder belts.

It is estimated that thousands of injuries can be prevented or reduced by the adoption of technological devices that provide protection in car crashes. In addition to seat belts, airbags, and approved safety seats for children, these technological changes would include side impact protection, rollover and fuel tank protection, frontal protection, and crashworthy seats.

*New York is the only state that adopted a school bus seat belt law. Don't you wonder about putting your children on school buses without seat belts?*

## Gun Control

Gunshot wounds to the head account for 150 million days of hospitalization a year for people between the ages of 1 and 34 years. Each year, nearly 400 children under the age of 15 are killed by handguns. There are children who accidently shoot themselves in the head playing with guns, and most recently, children have received head injuries because of drive-by shootings.

Gun control is a very explosive political topic wrapped up in individual rights. However, children are far too often the victims of liberal gun laws for adults. What are their rights for protection?

Alternatives to firearms as a means of personal protection should be developed and the legitimacy of violence as a means of solving problems examined. California has a law banning the sales of toy guns that are modeled after real guns. Children need to be taught that guns are not toys.

## Bike Helmets

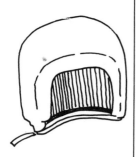

The use of bike helmets would go far to reduce and prevent brain injuries. Each year in the United States, nearly 600,000 persons are treated in emergency rooms and more than 1,300 die because of injuries sustained while riding a bicycle (Weiss 1991).

The death rate from bicycling injuries among children exceeds the death rate from many other causes that receive more public attention, such as accidental poisonings, falls, and firearm injuries. Yet little is done on a national level about bicycle-related deaths.

Currently, fewer than 10% of bicyclists use helmets when riding. It is estimated that, if all cyclists wore helmets, more than 2,500 deaths could have been prevented over a five-year period from 1984 through 1988. As importantly, it is estimated that over 300,000 head injuries could be prevented if 50% of cyclists wore helmets.

Awareness programs for children and parents would help increase helmet use. "It is now up to both individual health providers and those responsible for public safety to take this information and systematically implement programs designed to increase helmet use among bicyclists" (Weiss 1991, 3033).

## It Can Work! The Case of Three-Wheelers

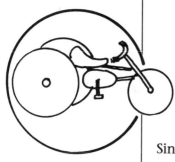

A few years ago, the Justice Department ruled that production of all-terrain three-wheelers be ceased because of the high rate of injury among children riding them. Numerous studies cited three-wheel accidents as an alarming etiology of injury and death (Kriel, Sheehan, Krach, Kriel and Rolewicz 1987; Smith and Middaugh 1986).

Since the Justice Department's ruling, most states have enacted laws that require education for drivers, helmets, and specific age limits for operation.

Using seat belts, keeping guns away from children, and bicycle helmets would go a very long way toward reducing injury in children.

An additional area to address legislatively is adults hurting children. This is the case with drunk driving and child abuse.

Changing behavior through health education is difficult, but possible. The injury prevention measures that have been most effective are well-enforced state laws mandating safe behavior.

# The Cost of Injury

It is difficult to find specific data relative to the economic burden of children being injured. Of course, the accident robs many of them of economic independence, not to mention the unbelievable cost of rehabilitation. As a backdrop for this section, the following cases are presented:

- Jake was born with an undiagnosed arterial-venous malformation in his brain which unexpectedly ruptured. He had a stroke at 15 months of age, and two neurosurgical procedures were needed to evacuate the bleeding.

  Currently he experiences right hemiplegia and blindness and functions cognitively at a two- to three-month level. Jake is the youngest of three children with supportive and loving parents. He has been in rehabilitation three weeks and the cost to date is $12,628.02.

- George is 7 years of age and received a severe head injury in a pedestrian/car accident. George has a tracheostomy and gastrostomy for all nutrition and hydration. He responds to some sensory information and is recently able to smile to tone of voice. He does not understand language and cannot speak. His current mental development is at a two- to three-month level.

  His mother is a single parent who has been unable to cope with his accident and thus rarely visits him. Hospital procedure requests are done through her attorney. George will likely be discharged to a nursing home if a space becomes available.

  It has been ten months since George's accident, and he has been in rehabilitative care for nine months. Rehabilitation cost to date is $248,136.59.

- Jenny is 8 years of age. She received a head injury in a bike/car accident. She was not wearing a helmet. She had neurosurgery to evacuate bleeding and to place a shunt because of hydrocephalus. Jenny has a tube in her nose because she is unable to drink enough fluid orally. However, she does eat orally.

She cannot speak because of brain stem damage. She is wheelchair-dependent and cognitively impaired. Current mental status is at a 4- to 5-year level. Jenny is the oldest of four children with loving, supportive parents. Her accident was four months ago, and she has been in rehabilitative care for three and a half months. Rehabilitation cost to date is $53,792.47.

- John, 7 years of age, received a suffocation anoxic injury in a construction accident when he fell in a hole and was covered by dirt. John is currently hypertonic and is unable to control this severe spasticity. He is wheelchair-dependent and is fed orally. He cannot speak and is learning to use a scanning communication system by directing his eye gaze.

  It is not possible to test John cognitively because he cannot control any of his movements. He does smile and laugh appropriately to language. John is the youngest of three boys with loving, supportive parents. His accident was six months ago and he has been in rehabilitation for five months. Rehabilitation cost to date is $103,169.87.

- Mike is a 17-year-old boy who received a severe closed head injury in a motor vehicle accident. He was not wearing a seat belt and was thrown from the car. He has a tracheostomy and gastrostomy. He is wheelchair-dependent. He can hear very loud sounds and will grimace when his face is tickled with a feather. He cannot see and is considered to be functionally comatose at this time.

  He is the second youngest of five children in a supportive, caring family. His accident was two and a half months ago, and he has been in rehabilitative care for five weeks. Rehabilitation cost to date is $38,872.35. In one week he will be discharged to a long-term care residence.

In 1987, Congress asked the National Highway Traffic Safety Administration to measure the cost of injury and associated disability in the United States. Researchers at the University of California-San Francisco and The Johns Hopkins University prepared *The Cost of Injury in the United States: A Report to Congress, 1989.* This report summarizes epidemiological information.

One of every four United States residents is injured every year. This amounts to 57 million persons of all ages and genders. Younger persons and males are the most affected. For every person killed, there are 16 people who are hospitalized for an injury.

The six leading causes of fatal injuries are motor vehicles, falls, firearms, poisonings, drowning, and fire. An injury is defined as damage to tissue caused by a transfer of energy or the absence of essentials, such as oxygen. (There are very high levels of kinetic energy released in car crashes, shootings, and falls. Chemical energy is the active agent in poisonings. Fires and scalding water release intolerably high levels of thermal energy. Submersion in water deprives the individual of oxygen required to maintain life.)

For 57 million injured people, the lifetime cost is an estimated $158 billion dollars. These figures are derived using the human capital approach. This method estimates losses resulting from death or disability by calculating lost productivity. When someone dies prematurely, society loses the benefits that it would have received if that individual had worked for the expected lifetime.

Society also loses when an individual is temporarily or permanently disabled by injury. These losses are termed indirect costs. Direct costs are actual dollar expenditures for medical and other related services, which make up 29% of the total lifetime costs. They include amounts spent for hospital and nursing home care, physician and other medical professional services, drugs, medical appliances, and rehabilitation.

The three most costly causes of injury incur cost in very different ways. Motor vehicle injuries cost $48.7 billion in lifetime costs, falls $37.3 billion, and firearms $14.4 billion. Yet the patterns of injury severity and thus the distribution of costs is quite distinct.

Firearm deaths account for 84% of all costs, due to the high mortality costs associated with deaths of young adults. Only 15% of the costs are associated with hospitalized injuries, and negligible costs are incurred by injuries not requiring hospitalization. A similar pattern is found for costs relating to drowning.

For falls, it is quite the opposite. Hospitalized injuries account for 80% of the total cost. These costs include medical and related services and the morbidity costs associated with disability following injury.

For motor vehicles, there is a more balanced contribution to costs by all three categories of injury severity, reflecting the significant numbers of people who die, who are hospitalized, and who are treated without hospitalization as a result of car crashes. Motor vehicle crashes cause $48.7 billion in lifetime costs.

These and other injuries cause private grief but do not necessarily produce only a private burden. In a case challenging the constitutionality of a motorcycle helmet law in Massachusetts, a lower court filed the following opinion which was affirmed by the United States Supreme Court:

> The public has an interest in minimizing the resources directly involved. From the moment of injury, society picks the person off the highway, delivers him to a municipal hospital and municipal doctors; provides him with unemployment compensation if, after recovery, he cannot replace his lost job and, if the injury causes permanent disability, may assume the responsibility for him and his family's subsistence. We do not understand a state of mind that permits plaintiff to think that only he himself is concerned. (*Injury Prevention Newsletter*, Fall 1990, 12)

The Report to Congress on the cost of injury estimates that a universal requirement that all motorcyclists wear a helmet would have a net benefit to society of $97 million a year.

Injuries can be prevented and minimized in severity. There are several tested strategies which are known to be effective in preventing deaths and injuries. Net savings are easily projected if these strategies were implemented on a national basis (*Injury Prevention Newsletter,* Fall 1990):

1. Airbags could save $4.7 billion. In 1984, the National Highway Traffic Safety Administration estimated a cost of $364 per car for full front-seat airbags. Not only would these airbags save cost, they would also save lives. It is projected that airbags would save 6,190 lives and prevent 110,360 serious injuries.

2. Driving licensure at age 17 could save $1.4 billion. In 1985, 2,014 people in the United States were killed in crashes involving 16-year-old drivers. If the minimum legal driving age were raised to 17, 1,375 deaths and 160,000 injuries could be avoided.

3. Elimination of high school driver education could save $863 million. Studies of the effectiveness of high school driver education have found little difference in risk of crash or injury when comparing driving records among those who did and did not participate in the program. However, it does result in large increases in early licensure in an age group with a very high crash rate. It is estimated that approximately 666 deaths and 72,000 injuries could be avoided by preventing early licensure due to driver education.

4. Bicycle helmet protection could save $183 million. Helmets have proven to be very effective in preventing head injuries among bicyclists. The cost of providing a helmet for every U.S. bicyclist would be $72 million.

The effectiveness of such a program was based on an Australian study. There, a helmet promotion campaign resulted in a 20% reduction in head injuries. Extrapolated to U.S. figures, this would result in 178 fewer deaths and 17,000 injuries that are much less severe. The savings, after deducting the cost of the free helmets, would be $183 million.

I t all seems so simple. Airbags, bike helmets, seat belts, and raising the driving age one year could effectively reduce the mortality and morbidity of brain injuries in children. It is so logical, such an easy solution. Yet this nation continues to place the dollars in the trauma and post-trauma care of these children. What an unusual prioritizing of dollars this is.

*Perhaps a personal anecdote could underscore the need for prevention. One and a half years ago, we chaired a committee to distribute 1,000 free bicycle helmets to graduating kindergartners in St. Paul, Minnesota. Funding was obtained, and on a beautiful Saturday afternoon in May 5-year-old children lined up to receive their free helmets.*

*We drove home from the project feeling so good, so hopeful that perhaps some children would now be spared the tragedy of injury. On the street was a 5-year-old girl balancing precariously on her new two-wheel bike with the new helmet firmly strapped to her head. The smiles on our faces were very broad indeed and lasted until Monday morning, when we went back to work on the rehabilitation unit for children with brain injuries.*

# 14

# Taking Care of You (While You're Taking Care of Others)

This chapter is for *you*—not the children and families you help. It is about taking care—not of them—of you!

Working with children who have had brain injuries winds us down sometimes. There are those days when we feel like the entire cast of the Wizard of Oz—we don't have the heart to care one more day; we don't have the brain to come up with one more creative therapy idea; and we don't have the courage to sit through one more family conference and report minimal progress.

We have come to recognize some of our more stressful times:

- when the children don't get better fast enough—and none of them ever get better fast enough, or completely enough!

- when our patient mix is skewed to the more severely injured child and progress is slow

- when we have to wade through a pile of messages to get to the children's charts on our desktops

- when the age of the injured child is close to that of our own children's

I would like to take this opportunity to provide some suggestions to help your stress level. They have helped me immensely. I call them, "from Carole Sellars' school of hard knocks," because I wish I had known these sooner in my career.

CAROLE W. SELLARS SCHOOL OF HARD KNOCKS

## The School of Hard Knocks

1. Get enough sleep! Not enough is ever said at stress workshops about the benefits of a good night's sleep. Sleep is essential to restore energy and clear thinking.

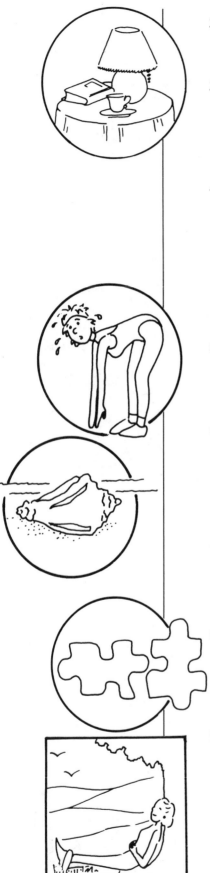

2. Read a good book. A good piece of fiction helps me transport myself into someone else's life. Reading before I go to sleep each night helps me forget me.

3. Take a break during the workday. This is a hypocritical suggestion, because I don't do it nearly as often as I should. But when I do take a brief walk outside, put my head down on my desk for a few minutes, or meditate in my office, I am refreshed and return with more verve!

4. Travel somewhere! This has been my personal obsession, and you may not agree. While travelling through many countries, I have learned a great deal about our own and somehow manage to find a more proper, balanced perspective of who I am in relation to my job. This means that travel provides humility for me. I return to work following these travel absences and find my department, the hospital, and, in fact, the country have functioned quite well without me! That is a comforting, humbling experience!

5. Exercise that body! My workout, three times a week—never any more, never any less—is my "cocktail" at the end of a busy day. My brain totally shuts down as my hamstrings kick in, and it always feels so very good . . . once it's **over!**

6. Another topic rarely discussed in professional texts and at conferences is one's own value system and how spirituality fits into healing. My church association provides me much in the way of structure to send healing prayers. Additionally, an hour of quiet each week gives me good reflective time, which is renewing to my energy reserve.

7. Some days you just have to muddle through! Give yourself permission to have days where you just keep putting one foot in front of the other. This "muddling" is a skill, maybe even an art. It is okay to have an average day. They can't all be brilliant.

8. Let some puzzles be unfinished! Candace and I spend too much time trying to figure out answers to our puzzles: why a dysarthria does not seem at all logical considering the site of lesion, or why some children remain unresponsive to language. These puzzles are inexplicable. It is okay to say, "I don't know!"

9. Don't just do something, sit there! For those of us who are compulsive maniacs in our energy output, please remember that it is permissible, in fact healthy, to sit and vegetate and relax and muse and think and daydream and fantasize and reminisce.

10. Get a cleaning person! This is something I wish I had done years sooner. In earlier days, I had to do it all perfectly, of course. Well, I don't anymore. So I have a cleaning person clean my home every two weeks, and I spend my energy on family and friendships rather than the toilet bowl!

11. Look at your leisure time, because no one on a death bed ever says, "I wish I had worked more!" This advice, from the minister of my church, has hit me many times where it counts—right in the ol' work ethic! I know I will be remembered for my contributions to family and friends, not my average daily charges or totally neat and organized desktop.

# Fight the Lions and Tigers

12. A few years ago, a story was told at a National Head Injury Foundation meeting about Mr. Buck, a world-famous animal trainer who had visited Africa many times to work with lions and tigers. At age 80 he was asked why he was no longer returning to Africa—was he afraid of the lions and tigers?

   Mr. Buck said he wasn't afraid of the lions and tigers, but he was terribly bothered by the gnats. As Africa became more developed and tourism increased, brush was cut back so people could view the lions and tigers. Swampland developed, and the gnats became a problem.

It is ironic, isn't it, to think of someone too bothered by the gnats to deal fearlessly with lions and tigers?

In conclusion, we would like to say that we hope you don't let the gnats get in the way of your fight. We all need to fight the "lions and tigers" for children with brain injuries: the fine tuning of clinical skills, the research to guide the future and explain the past, the capability and energy to prevent injuries, and the compassionate capacity to include so many people in the circle of your care.

Don't let the gnats get in your way: the rude family member, the impatient colleague, the guilt of neglected phone messages, and the tiresome requests to do things that take time from your clinical job—the budget, the educational plan, the quality assurance study.

We wish you continued success fighting your own lions and tigers —a fight undaunted by gnats!

# A Spiritual Look
## at a Career:
## What Recovering Children
## Have Taught Me

This was the first chapter I wrote for this book. I believe it reflects my increasing commitment to a topic never addressed at professional conferences, not even whispered about in family/team conferences, and certainly not included in professional texts on pediatric rehabilitation. This topic has to do with spirituality.

I suppose the absence of talking or writing about spirituality has to do with some deep-seated fear in all of us that it is too personal, certainly too unscientific, to include amidst discussions of videofluoroscopies, palatal lifts, and cognitive theories. And yet I strongly believe that my ability to assist in healing hurt children is *inextricably* bound to my own ability to heal myself.

This personal awareness has caused me to put away my clinical binoculars which focus on the child's recovery of speech and language, and step back with a wide-angle lens to view the whole panorama: the child, family, friends, my colleagues, and me. This new spiritual view has changed my view of the world.

## Definition of Spirituality

I would like to begin by defining how I would like to use the term *spiritual* in the context of this chapter. M. Scott Peck (1979) defines spirituality as "the force that pushes us as individuals and as a whole species to grow against the natural resistance of our own lethargy" (p. 268). Luke Skywalker, hero of "Star Wars," was right. This **force** needs to be with us all.

In this context, spirituality is the opposite of laziness. It is energy. It is work. It enables us all to overcome fear of a change in our comfortable security blanket of the status quo. It prods us to reach out to someone, pursue a dream, learn new information.

It follows, then, that this book is a spiritual relationship between author and reader. Candace and I have overcome lethargy (and not a small amount of anxiety) by writing it. You have overcome apathy by reading it, and it is our sincere wish that you have learned new information in the process.

# The Road Less Traveled

It is always spiritual work to heed that inner voice inside all of us that encourages taking the more difficult path, the road less traveled.

In the more specific context of this book, I have puzzled for years why so many people (therapists, educators, physicians, and nurses) have walked the career path of helping hurt children. What makes us do it? M. Scott Peck (1979) believes it is because we have chosen and been chosen by **grace.** I like that reason. It pleases me because I do know that the spiritual grace that led me to this career has serendipitously provided many gifts along the way.

We may have chosen a career because of its cognitive appeal but have found other gifts of grace as well. For me, these unexpected gifts have included laughter, intimacy, sadness, joy, poignancy, humility, and vulnerability. That is a lot to get from a mere job! For example, I am very grateful to work in an environment that, on a daily basis, provides me with gratitude for my own and loved ones' health. At the same time, I feel vulnerable facing the prospect that wellness is precarious and can end unexpectedly with an illness or accident.

These feelings of mine have led me on a quest. This is obviously a personal journey. I am not qualified on any level to teach spirituality. I only welcome the opportunity to share my journey and tell what I have learned.

The very first thing I have learned is that spiritual recovery is ignored at most hospitals, particularly rehabilitation centers. And yet what I have observed is that a frequent, unobtrusive visitor at the child's bedside is a minister, priest, or rabbi. Also, one of the first places the children go on that coveted first weekend pass home is church or synagogue. Churches hold prayer vigils for the children and participate in fund raising. These theological efforts seem ignored, however, within the walls of the hospital.

What feels wrong to me about this is that we are talking about *healing—whole-person healing.* As the fancy medical equipment and expertise shrouds these children, I have often asked, "How do these children heal? How does their spirit conquer? How do they answer that inevitable question, 'Why me?'"

My quest to find answers has led me, and many others, to Rabbi Kushner's book, *When bad things happen to good people* (1980). This book has answered my questions by stating that God does not will suffering. He does not cause these accidents to happen and children to get hurt. He is as sad as we all are when they do.

We all live in a world of danger. It is very difficult to accept the fact that there are no guarantees in life, no guarantees that life will progress as it should. Trust in this life does not mean trusting that life will always be good and free of grief and pain.

For me, a trust in life means believing that I have within me the spiritual energy to continue through life, regardless of what it brings. I have learned this lesson most poignantly from the families I have met at the hospital where I work. I have also met hundreds of children of all ages who have found that same capacity within themselves.

A few years ago Candace and I worked with a speech-language pathologist whose baby, Jack, was born prematurely, then diagnosed with cerebral palsy at ten months of age. We have been observers of her recovery—the ability to work through grief and anger to peace and the ability to find within herself the grace of acceptance.

We all have survived life's lessons. I have lost a younger brother to cancer and a dad to alcoholism while in his mid-fifties, and accepted a personal health problem. But nowhere have these lessons struck me with more force than working with families of children who have brain injuries.

One of the most serendipitous gifts I have received from my job is how quickly it puts in appropriate perspective the minor irritations of my life—a bout with the flu, a stalled car, an unexpected visitor to my department, phone-message notes. Around me are children who are daily battling pain, trusting me, moving forward. Somehow a head cold loses its power!

At social gatherings people are always saying to me, "How can you work *there?* You must have the patience of a saint!" This comment amuses me now. I am not at all a patient person—just ask any member of my family or friends! Somehow lay people assigning an adjective of patience to those of us in pediatric rehabilitation or to parents of children with disabilities diminishes the work we do. It implies that we are saintly not to berate a child impatiently who walks more slowly or speaks haltingly.

My personal experience is that I cannot wear the halo of a patient saint because the children I work with are living up to their capacity, trying hard, and giving it their all. If I switched careers to teaching required American literature to eighth-graders, perhaps I could wear that halo! In the meantime, I have learned to accept and be proud of my compassion. The pediatric clinical specialists I know can wear that adjective; and perhaps restructuring society's comment from "How can you be so patient?" to "How can you be so compassionate?" calls it as it is.

This has been a rather wordy introduction to the topic of spirituality. The question, of course, remains: How do we bring that inner strength, that spiritual energy, to the job? I would like to offer a few suggestions which have helped me connect with families and children.

# Ideas for Connecting Spiritually

1. **Tell the family and children how you *feel*.** For example, when I walk to a child's bed in the intensive care unit for the first time, I will say, "My name is Carole. I will be John's speech pathologist. I am very sorry he got hurt. How is he feeling today?" That is very different from, "My name is Carole. I will be John's speech pathologist. Can he follow commands yet?"

   Other feeling statements to families include: I am very sad Lisa's progress is so slow. I wish there was more I could do. William is a little better every time he goes home on a weekend pass. It does him so much good to be with his family, and that makes me happy.

   And, to the children: I am so sad you got hurt; I'm really angry at the person who hit you. You are so brave. You have so much courage. I love you. You try so hard every day—I am very proud of you and can't wait to tell your mom and dad how hard you work.

2. **Say good-bye properly.** I do this by taking children into a quiet office on their discharge day and telling them how very proud I am to have known someone so courageous. I tell them I will remember them always *(which I will!)* and thank them for being my friend. I also say these words to children unresponsive to language because it is important for *me* to say good-bye.

   I tell the parents how much they have taught me about love and acceptance and how many spiritual lessons I have learned from knowing them. After the child has been discharged and professional reports have been submitted, I send the parents a personal letter thanking them for the lessons they have taught me. And every parent has taught me something very valuable.

3. **If you are healing your wounds, get help.** It is my belief that in order to bring your true spiritual self to your job, professional help is needed when you are in personal pain. And none of us is immune to the personal pain of illness, death of a loved one, divorce, chemical dependency, or whatever. However, it is crucial to seek help when needed so that your hurt can heal and you, in turn, can help others.

4. **Offer the healing of the children in your care to a higher power.** I do this in church generally but have also done it in my car and my office. I imagine a very bright, warm, yellow light surrounding their faces and healing them. It only takes a moment, but it is an important lesson in humility because I do deeply believe that these outcomes are out of my control. Thus, I ask for help outside of me.

5. **Do something nice and anonymous.** We will vote as a department to send an anonymous gift to a child. Sometimes we choose a warm jacket or a warm toddler sleeper. Other times we will mail an outrageously impractical outfit or toy. Regardless of what the gift is, it makes us feel so good.

# Carole Sellars' Experiential Maxims

This is the fun part. I plan to hop on my soap box for a brief moment to talk about my opinions. These, too, are personal, and I would welcome comments. These opinions emerged from a paper I recently wrote on biomedical ethics, and after I finished the academic portion of my paper, these "maxims" literally flew onto the page. They were formed so quickly, I am convinced they have been in me for some time. I wrote them in response to our society's view of children as I perceive it.

1. **Quality of life need not be confused with the intelligence quotient.** It concerns me that prediction of quality of life is generally established to be cognitive abilities: speech, rational thought, memory, and language. But what about happiness and self-acceptance?

   I have come to believe that a child's reciprocal smile to loving care cements a bonding to family, teachers, therapists, and nurses. All of us waited impatiently for our own infants' first smile which, simply put, said, "Thank you." The anticipatory wiggle of a baby's body and smile of recognition makes the sleep deprivation bearable because the relationship finally becomes reciprocal.

   My experience is the children with disabilities who are able to smile in response to love, care, and attention give something back. And this smile reflects a cognitive age of two to three months. Over and over again, I have been part of that reciprocity and observed families bond to a smile. And, of course, laughter will simply cement a child in your heart forever! In my estimation, children with severe mental retardation who smile have a good quality of life. They are not unlike an infant who responds happily to attention, food, and stimulation.

   Much, much sadder lives can occur on the other end of the continuum—the child with an IQ of 85 to 100, less than one standard deviation below the mean. The learning differences may be secondary to mental retardation, learning disability, chronic epilepsy, or traumatic brain injury.

   Whatever the reason, these children are just far enough below the mean to be ignored and disconfirmed in the mainstream of school and life. They have few friends, and behavioral reactions of low self-esteem exacerbate isolation. I have cofacilitated support groups for adolescents recovering from brain injury who fit this description, and it has broken my heart to watch them struggle in the context of social indifference and isolation.

2. **Children with disabilities do not writhe in pain and agony.** My friends do not visit me at work. They say they are afraid to see children "suffering." Most people learn what I do for a job, smile awkwardly, and say, "I don't know **how** you can do it." Do what?—laugh, use my mind and creativity to teach others, be hugged, cry, smile, touch shoulders with my colleagues who share similar values, and get paid?

This is not an unhappy place. In my opinion, children with disabilities are not any more unhappy than their normal peers, perhaps less so. I do not see children writhing in endless suffering. That is not to say I don't see some very sad cases, but the vast majority of children I know are happy. So, please stop assuming that I work in a dismal dungeon!

3. **We'll never get the big picture.** Can our society learn to accept differences and not judge others according to their own personal projections? I see personal attitudes, media reports, and legal trends that seem so patronizing to those children with disabilities. There is a condescending attitude of sympathy and discomfort that says, "Oh, how can you bear it?"

We live in a contemporary society that creates special hospitals, special buses, special parking places, special schools, and special clinics for these special children. And then we train special people, like me, to work with these special children, but we don't want to hear about it at social gatherings. The attitude seems to be, "Let's try not to think about it. They should pull the plug; that's what I'd want for me." It's as though we attach the adjective "special" and it's okay.

But my premise is that *every* child is special, so the adjective quickly loses its "specialness." Every child in our society is simply a small citizen who depends on grown-ups—the homeless child, the cocaine-addicted child, the child with divorcing parents, the child scared at camp, the abducted child, the brilliant child, the raped child, the allergic child, the "sit on the bench all season" child, the yelled-at child, the hungry child, the shy child, the happy child, the disabled child.

All these children are ours, none more special than the other and all with an acute, frightening dependency on us grown-ups for affirmation, acceptance, and help. Nope, I believe our society will never get the big picture. One in four children in America lives below the poverty level, our infant mortality rate embarrasses all of us in health care, and biking helmets are unaffordable to low-income families. Nope, I believe our society will never get the big picture.

It's a tall order, advocating for children in this contemporary society of ours. Let us all recommit to this mission.

● ● ● ● ●

To me, it seems that youth is like a spring, an overpraised season— delightful if it happens to be a favored one, but in practice rarely favored and more remarkable, as a general rule, for biting east winds than genial breezes.

*–Samuel Butler*

Abraham Lincoln has said, "After 40 every man is responsible for his own face!" I passed that chronological milestone years ago, but I presume many of you still have the bloom of youth on yours. It is our concluding wish that all our faces are ones of gentleness, love, and strength, with just the right amount of laugh lines.

# References

Annegers, J. F. 1983. The epidemiology of head trauma in children. In *Pediatric head trauma*, edited by K. Shapiro, 1-10. New York: Futura Publishing.

Baker, S., B. O'Neil, and R. Karpf. 1984. *The injury fact book.* Lexington, MA: Lexington Books.

Barancik, J., B. Chatterjee, Y. Green, E. Mickenzi, and D. Fife. 1983. North-eastern Ohio trauma study: Magnitude of the problem. *American Journal of Public Health* 73:746-751.

Bell, W., D. Davis, A. Morgan-Fisher, and E. Ross. 1990. Acquired aprosodia in children. *Journal of Child Neurology* 5:19-26.

Bigler, E. 1987. Neuropathology of acquired cerebral trauma. *Journal of Learning Disabilities* 20:458-473.

Bloom, F., A. Lazerson, and L. Hofstadter. 1985. *Brain, mind, and behavior.* New York: W. H. Freeman and Co.

Boll, T. 1983. Minor head injury in children—Out of sight but not out of mind. *Journal of Clinical Child Psychology* 12(1):74-80.

Brink, J., A. Garrett, W. Hale, J. Woo-Sam, and V. Nickel. 1970. Recovery of motor and intellectual function in children sustaining severe head injuries. *Developmental Medicine and Child Neurology* 12:565-571.

Brink, J., C. Imbus, and J. Woo-Sam. 1980. Physical recovery after severe closed head trauma in children and adolescents. *Journal of Pediatrics* 97(5):721-727.

Brookshire, R. 1973. *An introduction to aphasia.* Minneapolis, MN: BRK Publishers.

Butler, N., and J. Golding, eds. 1986. *From birth to five: A study of the health and behavior of Britain's five year olds.* New York: Pergamon Press.

Center for Disease Control. 1982. Blood alcohol concentration among young drivers: United States—1982. *MMWR Publication 1983* 32:646-648.

Cohen, S. 1991. Adapting educational programs for students with head injuries. *The Journal of Head Trauma Rehabilitation* 6(1):56-63.

Dodson, F., and A. Alexander. 1986. *Your child: Birth to age 6.* New York: Simon and Schuster.

Ewing-Cobbs, L., and J. Fletcher. 1987. Neuropsychological assessment of head injury in children. *Journal of Learning Disabilities* 20(9):526-535.

Farmer, M., H. Singer, E. Millits, D. Hall, and E. Charney. 1987. Neurobehavioral sequelae of minor head injuries in children. *Pediatric Neuroscience* 13:304-308.

Feldman, K. 1980. Prevention of childhood accidents: Recent programs. *Pediatrics in Review* 2(3):75-81.

Filly, C., J. Cranberg, M. Alexander, and E. Hart. 1987. Neurobehavioral outcome after closed head injury in childhood and adolescence. *Archives of Neurology* 44:194-198.

Fowles, B., and M. Glanz. 1976. Competence and talent in verbal riddle comprehension. *Journal of Child Language* 4:433-452.

Franklin, J. 1987. *Molecules of the mind.* New York: Atheneum.

Fuld, P., and P. Fisher. 1977. Recovery of intellectual ability after closed head injury. *Developmental Medicine and Child Neurology* 19:495-502.

Giebink, G. (Fall) 1986. Unpublished paper presented at the American Academy of Pediatrics. *Minnesota Pediatrician.*

Gilling, D., and R. Brightwell. 1982. *The human brain.* New York: Facts on File.

Jacobson, M., E. Rubenstein, W. Bohannon, D. Sondheimer, R. Cicci, J. Toner, E. Gong, and F. Heald. 1986. Follow-up of adolescent trauma victims: A new model of care. *Pediatrics* 77(2):326-341.

Jennett, B. 1986. The future role of neurosurgery in the care of head injuries. *Neurosurgery Review* 9:129-133.

Jennett, B., and F. Plum. 1972. Persistent vegetative state after brain injury: A syndrome in search of a name. *Lancet* 4:743-747.

Jennett, B., and D. Teasdale. 1981. *Management of head injuries.* Contemporary Neurology Series 20. Philadelphia: Davis.

Kail, R. 1990. *The development of memory in children.* New York: W. H. Freeman and Co.

Klonhoff, H. 1971. Head injuries in children: Predisposing factors, accident conditions, accident proneness, and sequelae. *American Journal of Public Health* 61:2405-2417.

Klonhoff, H., G. Low, and C. Clark. 1977. Head injuries in children: A prospective five year follow-up. *Journal of Neurology, Neurosurgery, and Psychiatry* 40:1211-1219.

Kraus, J., D. Fife, and P. Cox. 1986. Incidence, severity, and external causes of pediatric brain injury. *American Journal of Diseases of Childhood* 140:687-693.

Kriel, R., L. Krach, and L. Panser. 1989. Closed head injury: Comparison of children younger and older than 6 years of age. *Pediatric Neurology* 5(5):296-300.

Kriel, R., L. Krach, and M. Sheehan. 1984. Preliminary findings. Pediatric brain injury study, Gillette Children's Hospital, St. Paul, MN.

Kriel, R., M. Sheehan, L. Krach, H. Kriel, and T. Rolewicz. 1987. Pediatric head injury from all-terrain vehicle accidents. *Pediatrics* 78:933-935.

Kriel, R., M. Sheehan, and L. Krach. 1986. Pediatric head injury resulting from all-terrain vehicle accidents. *Pediatrics* 78:933-935.

Kushner, H. 1980. *When bad things happen to good people.* New York: Schoken Books.

League of Women Voters of Minnesota. 1987. *Health care for Minnesota's children: Investing in the future.* Minneapolis, MN: League of Women Voters of Minnesota Education Fund.

Lehr, E. 1990. *Psychological management of traumatic brain injuries in children.* Rockville, MD: Aspen.

Levin, H., H. Eisenberg, N. Wigg, and K. Kobayashi. 1982. Memory and intellectual ability after head injury in children and adolescents. *Neurosurgery* 11(5):668-673.

McGhee, P. 1970. Children's appreciation of humor: A test of the cognitive congruency principle. *Child Development* 47:420-426.

McGhee, P., and J. Goldstein, eds. 1983. *Handbook of humor research. Volume I: Basic issues; Volume II: Applied studies.* New York: Springer-Verlag.

Mahoney, W., J. D'Souza, J. Haller, M. Rogers, H. Epstein, and J. Freeman. 1983. Long-term outcome of children with severe head trauma and prolonged coma. *Pediatrics* 7(5):756-762.

Mencel, S. 1991. *I'm a parent of a school age child with a head/brain injury. How can I work with the school?* St. Paul, MN: Minnesota Head Injury Association.

Miller, C., A. Fine, and J. Adams-Taylor. 1989. *Monitoring children's health: Key indicators.* 2nd ed. Washington, DC: American Public Health Association.

Mitchell, D., and P. Stone. 1973. Temporal bone fractures in children. *Canadian Journal of Otolaryngology* 2(2):156-162.

National Center for Health Statistics. 1987. Advance report: Final mortality statistics. In *Monthly Vital Statistics Report* 31:6. Suppl. (DHHS Publ. No. PHS 82-1120). Hyattsville, MD: U.S. Public Health Service.

National Highway Traffic Safety Administration. 1989. *The cost of injury in the United States: A report to Congress.* Washington, DC.

National Safety Council. 1984. *Accident Facts.* 1984. Washington, DC.

Netter, F. H. 1989. *Atlas of human anatomy.* Ardsley, NY: CIBA-GEIGY Corp.

NIDRR National pediatric trauma registry: A progress report. Summer/Fall, 1991. *Rehabilitation Update* 4-5.

Orlowski, J. 1987. Drowning, near drowning, and ice water submersions. *Pediatric Clinic of North America* 34(1):183-192.

Peck, M. 1979. *The road less traveled.* New York: Simon and Schuster.

Pierce, J., D. Lyle, S. Quine, N. Evans, J. Morris, and M. Fearnside. 1990. The effectiveness of coma arousal intervention. *Brain Injury* 4(2):191-197.

Pulaski, M. 1980. *Understanding Piaget.* New York: Harper and Row.

Raimondi, A., and J. Hirschauer. 1989. Head injury in the infant and toddler. *Child's Brain* 11:12-35.

Rancho Los Amigos Hospital. 1979. *Rehabilitation of the head injured adult: Comprehensive physical management.* Downey, CA.

Restak, R. 1991. *The brain has a mind of its own.* New York: Harmony Books.

Savage, R. 1991. Identification, classification, and placement issues for children with traumatic brain injuries. *Journal of Head Trauma Rehabilitation* 6(1):1-9.

_____. 1992. Minutes of the pediatric task force meeting, National Head Injury Foundation meeting, Los Angeles, CA.

Shephard, S. 1989. Immersion injury: Drowning and near drowning. *Postgraduate Medicine* 85(8):183-192.

Smith, S., and J. Middaugh. 1986. Injuries associated with three-wheeled, all terrain vehicles, Alaska, 1983 and 1984. *Journal of the American Medical Association* 255:2454-2458.

Splaingar, M., D. Gaebler, P. Havens, and M. Kalichman. 1989. Brain injury: Functional outcome in children with tracheostomies and gastrostomies. *Archives of Physical Medicine and Rehabilitation* 70:318-321.

Springer, S., and G. Deutach. 1981. *Left brain, right brain.* New York: W. H. Freeman and Co.

Stover, S., and H. Zeiger. 1976. Head injury in children and teenagers. Functional recovery correlated with the duration of coma. *Archives of Physical Medicine and Rehabilitation* 57:201-205.

Teasdale, G., and B. Jennett. 1974. Assessment of coma and impaired consciousness. *Lancet* 2:81-84.

Telzrow, C. 1987. Management of academic and educational problems in head injury. *Journal of Learning Disabilities* 20(9):536-545.

United States Department of Health and Human Services, Office of Human Development Services, Administration for Children, Youth and Families. National Center on Child Abuse and Neglect. 1980. *Study of national incidence and prevalence of child abuse and neglect.* Washington, DC.

Vachss, A. 1982. Child abuse: A ticking bomb. *Change* 5(3):6.

Weiss, B., ed. 1991. Bicycle helmets: Effective but underused. *Journal of the American Medical Association* 266(21):3032-3033.

Wilson, S., G. Powell, K. Elliott, and H. Thwaites. 1991. Sensory stimulation in prolonged coma: Four single case studies. *Brain Injury* 5(4):393-400.

Ylvisaker, M., P. Hartwick, and M. Stevens. 1991. School reentry following head injury: Managing the transition from hospital to school. *Journal of Head Trauma Rehabilitation* 6(1):10-22.

Zigler, E., and J. Levine. 1967. Cognitive challenge as a factor in children's humor appreciation. *Journal of Personality and Social Psychology* 6(3):332-336.

Zillman, D., B. Williams, J. Bryant, K. Boynton, and M. Wolf. 1980. Acquisition of information from educational television programs as a function of differently paced humorous inserts. *Journal of Educational Psychology* 72(2):170-180.

# Appendixes

## A. Levels of Consciousness

Summary Sheet (reproducible)

Record of Consciousness Levels, Infants (6 Months to 2 Years)
   (reproducible)

Record of Consciousness Levels, Preschool (2 to 5 Years)
   (reproducible)

Record of Consciousness Levels, School Age (5 Years and Older)
   (reproducible)

Speech Pathology Therapy at the Six Levels of Consciousness
   (reproducible)

Physical and Occupational Therapy at the Six Levels of
   Consciousness (reproducible)

## B. Suggested Tests and Assessment Tools

Intelligence Tests

Speech and Language Tests

Perceptual Motor Skills Tests

Cognitive/Achievement Tests

Assessment of Young Children

## C. Suggested Language and Cognitive Activities

Commercially Available Workbooks

Catalogs

Computer Software

Computer Peripherals

# Appendix A
# Levels of Consciousness

## Summary Sheet

**Level 5:** **No response to stimuli**
Patient as presents in emergency room

**Level 4:** **Generalized response to sensory stimuli**
Response to pain:
Reflex withdrawal
Facial grimace
Response to sound before vision (usually)

**Level 3:** **Localized response to sensory stimuli**
Visual:     Blinking to light or threat, then eye following
More optimistic outcome, especially if displays visual responses
Movement of extremities: Localized response

### *** Official End of Comatose Period ***

**Level 2:** **Responsive to environment**
Purposeful activity
Following commands—Use gestures as well as verbal

**Level 1: Oriented to self and surroundings**
Oriented to time and place

**Level 0: Return to pre-accident status**

Adapted from Brink, Imbus, and Woo-Sam 1980.

# Record of Consciousness Levels for Head Trauma Patients
## Infants (6 Months to 2 Years)

Directions: Check all behaviors as present (+) or absent (–) on each date tested.

| Name:_____ Test Dates: | | | | | | | | |
|---|---|---|---|---|---|---|---|---|
| **Level 5: No response to stimuli** | | | | | | | | |
| Complete absence of observable change in behavior to visual, auditory, or painful stimuli | | | | | | | | |
| **Level 4: Gives generalized response to sensory stimuli** | | | | | | | | |
| Gives generalized startle to loud sound | | | | | | | | |
| Responds to repeated auditory stimulation with increased or decreased activity | | | | | | | | |
| Gives generalized reflex response to painful stimuli | | | | | | | | |
| **Level 3: Gives localized response to sensory stimuli** | | | | | | | | |
| Blinks when strong light crosses field of vision | | | | | | | | |
| Follows moving object passed within visual field | | | | | | | | |
| Turns toward or away from loud sound | | | | | | | | |
| Gives localized response to painful stimuli | | | | | | | | |
| **Level 2: Demonstrates awareness of environment** | | | | | | | | |
| Responds to name | | | | | | | | |
| Recognizes mother or other family members | | | | | | | | |
| Enjoys imitative vocal play | | | | | | | | |
| Giggles or smiles when talked to or played with | | | | | | | | |
| Fussing is quieted by soft voice or touch | | | | | | | | |
| **Level 1: Interacts with environment** | | | | | | | | |
| Shows active interest in toys; manipulates or examines before mouthing or discarding | | | | | | | | |
| Watches other children at play; may move toward them purposefully | | | | | | | | |
| Initiates social contact with adults; enjoys socializing | | | | | | | | |
| Shows active interest in bottle | | | | | | | | |
| Reaches or moves toward person or object | | | | | | | | |

Adapted from Levels of Consciousness Record, Pediatric Brain Injury Service, Rancho Los Amigos Hospital, Downey, California

# Record of Consciousness Levels for Head Trauma Patients
## Preschool (2 to 5 Years)

Directions: Check all behaviors as present (+) or absent (−) on each date tested.

Name:_____  Test Dates: | | | | | | | | |

| | | | | | | | | |
|---|---|---|---|---|---|---|---|---|

**Level 5: No response to stimuli**

| Complete absence of observable change in behavior to visual, auditory, or painful stimuli | | | | | | | | | |
|---|---|---|---|---|---|---|---|---|---|

**Level 4: Gives generalized response to sensory stimuli**

| | | | | | | | | | |
|---|---|---|---|---|---|---|---|---|---|
| Gives generalized startle to loud sound | | | | | | | | | |
| Responds to repeated auditory stimulation with increased or decreased activity | | | | | | | | | |
| Gives generalized reflex response to painful stimuli | | | | | | | | | |

**Level 3: Gives localized response to sensory stimuli**

| | | | | | | | | | |
|---|---|---|---|---|---|---|---|---|---|
| Blinks when strong light crosses field of vision | | | | | | | | | |
| Follows moving object passed within visual field | | | | | | | | | |
| Turns toward or away from loud sound | | | | | | | | | |
| Gives localized response to painful stimuli | | | | | | | | | |

**Level 2: Demonstrates awareness of environment**

| | | | | | | | | | |
|---|---|---|---|---|---|---|---|---|---|
| Follows simple commands | | | | | | | | | |
| Refuses to follow commands by shaking head or saying "no" | | | | | | | | | |
| Imitates examiner's gestures or facial expressions | | | | | | | | | |
| Responds to name | | | | | | | | | |
| Recognizes mother or other family members | | | | | | | | | |
| Enjoys imitative vocal play | | | | | | | | | |

**Level 1: Oriented to self and surroundings**

| | | | | | | | | | |
|---|---|---|---|---|---|---|---|---|---|
| Provides accurate information about self | | | | | | | | | |
| Is aware of being away from home | | | | | | | | | |
| Knows where toys, clothes, and other objects are kept | | | | | | | | | |
| Actively participates in treatment program | | | | | | | | | |
| Recognizes own room, knows way to bathroom, nursing station, etc. | | | | | | | | | |
| Is potty-trained | | | | | | | | | |
| Shows active interest in toys; will examine or manipulate before mouthing or discarding | | | | | | | | | |
| Watches other children at play; may move toward them purposefully to watch or snatch toy | | | | | | | | | |
| Initiates social contact with adult. Enjoys socializing. | | | | | | | | | |

Adapted from Levels of Consciousness Record, Pediatric Brain Injury Service, Rancho Los Amigos Hospital, Downey, California

# Record of Consciousness Levels for Head Trauma Patients
## School Age (5 Years and Older)

Directions: Check all behaviors as present (+) or absent (−) on each date tested.

| Name:_____ Test Dates: | | | | | | | | | |
|---|---|---|---|---|---|---|---|---|---|
| **Level 5: No response to stimuli** | | | | | | | | | |
| Complete absence of observable change in behavior to visual, auditory, or painful stimuli | | | | | | | | | |
| **Level 4: Gives generalized response to sensory stimuli** | | | | | | | | | |
| Gives generalized startle to loud sound | | | | | | | | | |
| Responds to repeated auditory stimulation with increased or decreased activity | | | | | | | | | |
| Gives generalized reflex response to painful stimuli | | | | | | | | | |
| **Level 3: Gives localized response to sensory stimuli** | | | | | | | | | |
| Blinks when strong light crosses field of vision | | | | | | | | | |
| Follows moving object passed within visual field | | | | | | | | | |
| Turns toward or away from loud sound | | | | | | | | | |
| Gives localized response to painful stimuli | | | | | | | | | |
| **Level 2: Is responsive to environment** | | | | | | | | | |
| Follows simple verbal or gestured requests | | | | | | | | | |
| Initiates purposeful activity | | | | | | | | | |
| Actively participates in therapy program | | | | | | | | | |
| Refuses to follow request by shaking head or saying "no" | | | | | | | | | |
| Imitates examiner's gestures or facial expressions | | | | | | | | | |
| **Level 1: Oriented to time and place; is recording ongoing events** | | | | | | | | | |
| Can provide accurate, detailed information about self and present situation | | | | | | | | | |
| Knows way to and from daily activities | | | | | | | | | |
| Knows sequence of daily routine | | | | | | | | | |
| Knows way around ward; recognizes own room | | | | | | | | | |
| Can find own bed; knows where personal belongings are kept | | | | | | | | | |
| Is bowel and bladder trained | | | | | | | | | |

Adapted from Levels of Consciousness Record, Pediatric Brain Injury Service, Rancho Los Amigos Hospital, Downey, California

# Speech Pathology Therapy
# at the Six Levels of Consciousness

## Emphasis: Return of Cognitive and Communication Skills

### Level 5: No response to stimuli
The team speech pathologist is not involved with the patient at this level.

### Level 4: Generalized response to sensory stimuli
1. Participates in team sensory stimulation program (along with PT, OT, and nursing staff):
   a. to prevent sensory deprivation
   b. to elicit responses
2. Evaluates consistency of response to determine an organized and meaningful stimulation program
3. Educates family about recovery and treatment procedures

   *Main Goals:*  To prevent sensory deprivation and elicit responses

   To design an organized program of stimulation that elicits consistent responses

### Level 3: Localized response to sensory stimulation
1. Sensory stimulation program to:
   a. elicit responses
   b. channel responses to purposeful activity
2. Provide a *meaningful* stimulation program based on family input
3. Assess the child's emerging *attention* responses
4. Facilitate visual and auditory attention and stimulus/response capabilities through the use of adapted switches on the microcomputer
5. Arrange an audiology consult to assess auditory localization responses
6. Assess spontaneous vocalizations, function of oral musculature, and speech production capabilities
7. Continue family education
8. Early planning for hospital discharge
9. Orientation to reality
10. Evaluate ability to make binary choices

   *Main Goals:*  Channel responses to purposeful activity

   Evaluate auditory responses

   Evaluate emerging speech production capabilities

### Level 2: Responsive to environment: Structure dependent
1. Continue orientation to reality
2. Introduce microcomputer software that encourages participation and provides structure
3. Elicit attention to task
4. Elicit imitation of activities—verbal/nonverbal
5. Evaluate speech production capabilities

6. Assess recent memory
7. Administer baseline language measures to assess current status and specific modality strengths and weaknesses
8. Determine need for augmentative or assistive speech and language system
9. Evaluate vocal quality disorders and implications for treatment
10. Continue family teaching
11. Gather information on patient's function during weekend passes

*Main Goals:* Facilitate cognitive recovery as it relates to language and memory

Facilitate recovery of speech production capabilities

Maximize structure to provide highest level of responding

### Level 1: Patient is oriented to self and surroundings: Concrete processing

1. Reduce structure to encourage independence
2. Introduce treatment activities and computer software to facilitate return of cognitive skills:
   a. discrimination
   b. classification
   c. memory
   d. conceptualization
   e. association
   f. analysis
   g. problem solving and inference
3. Evaluate novel learning
4. Evaluate and provide activities to facilitate judgment
5. Continue speech production program
6. Introduce activities to facilitate return to the classroom and family
7. Administer speech and language test battery to evaluate the need for local therapy, identify the nature of residual deficits, and determine an appropriate follow-up test protocol
8. Instruct patient in neurological recovery process and the nature of the residual deficits

*Main Goals:* Encourage independence by reducing structure

Continued facilitation of cognitive and language recovery

Continued facilitation of speech production recovery

Identification of residual deficits

Integration to home/school/community

### Level 0: Return to pre-accident status

Adapted from original material developed at Gillette Children's Hospital, Speech Pathology Department, June, 1984

# Physical and Occupational Therapy
# at the Six Levels of Consciousness

**Level 5: No response to stimuli**

1. Range of motion
2. Positioning

   *Main Goals:*  Prevention of contractures and skin problems

   Assessment of sensory responsiveness

**Level 4: Generalized response to sensory stimuli**

1. Range of motion
2. Adaptive equipment needs
3. Begin to monitor orthotic and/or casting needs
4. Sensory stimulation
5. Family education about recovery and treatment procedures

   *Main Goals:*  Prevention of sensory deprivation and elicitation of responses

   Prevention of contractures and skin problems

**Level 3: Localized response to sensory stimuli**

1. Range of motion
2. Update adaptive equipment needs
3. Monitor orthotics/casting
4. Sensory stimulation—task-oriented approach
5. Facilitate basic motor skills
6. Initiate progression of feeding program
7. Continue family education
8. Address identified needs from weekend pass information
9. Early planning for hospital discharge

   *Main Goals:*  Channel appropriate responses into purposeful activity

   Facilitate motor control

   Prevent contractures and skin problems

**Level 2: Responsive to environment—Follows gestured or verbal commands**

1. Monitor range of motion
2. Update adaptive equipment needs
3. Monitor orthotics/casting
4. Patient participation in reacquisition of sensory motor abilities
5. Self-care training
6. Integration of cognitive skills and motor tasks
7. Continued family education
8. Continue to address identified needs from weekend pass information
9. Continue discharge planning

   *Main Goal:*  Facilitation of sensory motor abilities for functional use

**Level 1: Patient is oriented to self and surroundings**

1. Update adaptive equipment needs
2. Monitor orthotics/casting
3. Continue emphasis on reacquisition of sensory motor abilities
4. Integration of cognitive skills and motor tasks
5. Formal and informal assessment
6. Facilitation and integration to home/school/community
7. Continued family education

   *Main Goals:*  Continued facilitation to cognitive and motor recovery

   Integration to home/school/community

**Level 0: Return to pre-injury status**

Adapted from original material developed at Gillette Children's Hospital, Physical and Occupational Therapy Department, June, 1984

# Appendix B
# Suggested Tests and
# Assessment Tools*

## Intelligence Tests

Detroit Test of Learning Aptitude-2 (DTLA-2)
Hammill, D. D.
Pro-Ed
8700 Shoal Creek Blvd.
Austin, TX 78758

Kaufman Assessment Battery for Children (K-ABC)
American Guidance Service
Circle Pines, MN 55014

Pictorial Test of Intelligence (PTI) French
The Riverside Publishing Co.
8420 Bryn Mawr Ave.
Chicago, IL 60631

Stanford-Binet Intelligence Scale: Fourth Edition
The Riverside Publishing Co.
8420 Bryn Mawr Ave.
Chicago, IL 60631

Wechsler Preschool and Primary Scale of Intelligence (WPPSI)
Wechsler Intelligence Scale for Children—Revised (WISC-R)
The Psychological Corp.
555 Academic Court
San Antonio, TX 78204

## Speech and Language Tests

Clinical Evaluation of Language Fundamentals—Revised
Charles E. Merrill Publishing Co.
Bell and Howell Co.
Columbus, OH 43216

*From *Assessment. Special education tests. A handbook for parents and professionals.* PACER Center,
4826 Chicago Avenue South, Minneapolis, MN, 55417-1055

Expressive One-Word Picture Vocabulary Test—Revised
(EOWPVT-R)
Academic Therapy Publications
20 Commercial Blvd.
Novato, CA 94947

Goldman-Fristoe Test of Articulation (GFTA)
American Guidance Service
Circle Pines, MN 55014

Peabody Picture Vocabulary Test—Revised (PPVT-R)
American Guidance Service
Circle Pines, MN 55014

Test of Language Development—Primary (TOLD-P)
Pro-Ed
8700 Shoal Creek Blvd.
Austin, TX 78758

The Word Test
LinguiSystems
Suite 806
1630 5th Ave.
Moline, IL 61265

## Perceptual Motor Skills Tests

Bruininks-Oseretsky Test of Motor Proficiency
American Guidance Service
Circle Pines, MN 55014

Developmental Test of Visual-Motor Integration (VMI)
Beery, K. E.
Modern Curriculum Press
Cleveland, OH

Motor Free Visual Perception Test (MVPT)
Academic Therapy Publications, Inc.
28 Commercial Blvd.
Novato, CA 94947

## Cognitive/Achievement Tests

Wide Range Achievement Test—Revised (WRAT-R)
Jastak Assessment Systems
Wilmington, DE

Woodcock-Johnson Psycho-Educational Battery—Revised (WJ-R)
DLM/Teaching Resources
P.O. Box 4000
One DLM Park
Allen, TX 75002

## Assessment of Young Children

Bayley Scales of Infant Development
Bayley, Nancy
Psychology Corp.
Harcourt, Brace, Jovanovich, Inc.
P.O. Box 839954
San Antonio, TX 78283

Hawaii Early Learning Profile (HELP)
VORT Corp.
P.O. Box 60132
Palo Alto, CA 94306

Leiter International Performance Scale
Slosson Educational Publishers, Inc.
P.O. Box 280
Aurora, NY 14052

Preschool Language Scale-3
Zimmerman, I. L., V. G. Steiner, and R. E. Pond
Psychology Corp.
Harcourt, Brace, Jovanovich, Inc.
P.O. Box 839954
San Antonio, TX 78283

Receptive-Expressive Emergent Language Scale (REEL-2)
Bzoch, K. R., and R. League
Slosson Educational Publishers, Inc.
P.O. Box 280
E. Aurora, NY 14052

Sequenced Inventory of Communication Development (SICD-R)
Hedrick, D. L., E. M. Prather, and A. P. Tobin
Slosson Educational Publishers, Inc.
P.O. Box 280
E. Aurora, NY 14052

# Appendix C
# Suggested Language and Cognitive Activities

## Commercially Available Workbooks

*Handbook of exercises for language processing* (Vols. I and II)
Lazzari, M., and P. M. Peters
LinguiSystems, Inc.
Suite 806
1630 Fifth Avenue
Moline, IL 61265

*Language rehabilitation: Auditory comprehension*
Martinoff, J. T., R. Martinoff, and V. Stokke
C.C. Publications, Inc.
P.O. Box 23699
Tigard, OR 97223

*Language rehabilitation: Verbal expression*
Martinoff, J. T., R. Martinoff, and V. Stokke
C. C. Publications, Inc.
P.O. Box 23699
Tigard, OR 97223

*Language remediation and expansion: 100 skill-building
reference lists*
Bush, C. S.
Communication Skill Builders, Inc.
3830 E. Bellevue
Tucson, AZ 85716

*Manual of exercises for expressive reasoning*
Zachman, L., C. Jorgenson, M. Barrett, R. Huisingh, and M. Snedden
LinguiSystems, Inc.
Suite 806
1630 Fifth Avenue
Moline, IL 61265

*The thinking skills workbook: A cognitive skills remediation manual for adults*
Tondat Carter, L., J. L. Caruso, M. A. Languirand, and M. A. Berard
Charles C. Thomas, Publisher
Springfield, IL 62794

*Workbook for aphasia: Exercises for the redevelopment of higher level language functioning*
Brubaker, S.
Wayne State University Press
Royal Oak, MI 48072

*Workbook for reasoning skills. Exercises for cognitive facilitation*
Brubaker, S.
William Beaumont Hospital
Wayne State University Press
Royal Oak, MI 48072

## Catalogs

American Guidance Service
4201 Woodland Road
Circle Pines, MN 55014-1796
(612) 786-4343

Communication Skill Builders
3830 E. Bellevue
Tucson, AZ 85716
(602) 323-7500

DLM Catalog
One DLM Park
Allen, TX 75002
1-800-527-4747

Edmark Corporation
P.O. Box 3903
Bellevue, WA 98009-3903

Educational Resources
1550 Executive Drive
Elgin, IL 60123
1-800-624-2926

HUMOResources
The HUMOR Project, Inc.
110 Spring Street
Saratoga Springs, NY 12866
(518) 587-8770

Minnesota Educational Computer Corporation (MECC)
3490 Lexington Avenue North
St. Paul, MN 55126

Slosson Educational Publications, Inc.
P.O. Box 280
East Aurora, NY 12866
(518) 587-8770

Sunburst Communications/WINGS for Learning
1600 Green Hills Road
P.O. Box 660002
Scotts Valley, CA 95067-0002


## Computer Software

Brøderbund
*Bankstreet Writer*®
*McGee* ®
*McGee Visits Katie's Farm*®
*Where in the U.S.A. Is Carmen Sandiego?*®
*Where in the World Is Carmen Sandiego?*®

Communication Skill Builders
*Exploratory Play* (uses Muppet Learning Keys™)
*Multiple Meanings*
*Representational Play* (uses Muppet Learning Keys™)

Methods & Solutions, Inc.
*Ace Inquirer*™
*Ace Reporter*™

Optimum Resource, Inc.
*Stickybear*® *ABC*
*Stickybear*® *Opposites*
*Stickybear*® *Reading*
*Stickybear*® *Shapes*

Spinnaker Software Corporation
*Facemaker*™
*Story Machine*™

The Learning Company
*Gertrude's Secrets*®
*Think Quick!*®

Minnesota Education Computer Corporation
*The Oregon Trail*™
*Word Munchers*™
*Zoyon Patrol*™

Sunburst Communications/WINGS for Learning
*Factory*™
*Gears*™
*Iggy's Gnees*™
*Memory Building Blocks*™
*Memory Castle*™
*Royal Rules*™
*Teddy's Playground*™
*What's in a Frame?*™

## Computer Peripherals

Muppet Learning Keys™
Sunburst Communications/WINGS for Learning
1600 Green Hills Road
P.O. Box 660002
Scotts Valley, CA 95067-0002

PowerPad™
Dunamis, Inc.
(Available from Don Johnson Developmental Equipment, Inc., P.O. Box 6539, 1000 N. Rand Road, Bldg. 115, Wauconda, IL, 60084)

TouchWindow®
Edmark Corporation
6727 - 185th Ave. N.E.
P.O. Box 3218
Redmond, WA 98073-3218

### Speech Synthesizers

Both of the speech synthesizers listed below are available from the Edmark Corporation, 6727 - 185th Ave. N.E., P.O. Box 3218, Redmond, WA, 98073-3218.

ECHO® Speech Processors
Street Electronics

Speech Thing®
Covox, Inc.

*Meet your therapy goals using these great products . . .*

### PHOTO CUE CARDS
**300 Meaningful Pictures for Oral Language Practice**
*by J. Y. K. Kerr*

These six 50-card sets present photographs of real-life objects, people, and activities. You can teach language structures and functions—and build vocabulary. This practical material adapts to your therapy approach. You'll have 300 quality photo cards to choose from.   **Catalog No. 4650-Y      $89**

### MORE PHOTO CUE CARDS
**300 New Pictures for Oral Language Practice**

If you like *Photo Cue Cards,* you'll love the sequel! These six card sets present exciting new photographs of real-life objects, people, and activities. Use them alone or along with *Photo Cue Cards* to teach language structures and functions, and build vocabulary. This practical material adapts to your therapy approach. You'll have 300 quality photo cards to choose from.

**Catalog No. 7532-Y      $89**

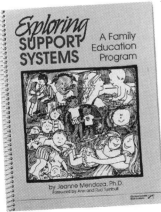

### EXPLORING SUPPORT SYSTEMS
**A Family Education Program**
*by Jeanne Mendoza, Ph.D.*

Help families of high-risk, handicapped, recently diagnosed, or at-risk infants, toddlers, and preschoolers build support systems with this comprehensive manual. Lead families through a series of six sessions and follow up with a seventh home visit. Sessions address the types of stress that family members may face and explore available support systems. You'll have instructor and parent materials in one convenient, completely reproducible manual.   **Catalog No. 7768-Y      $39**

### PLANNING FAMILY GOALS
**A Systems Approach to the IFSP**
*by Jennifer Olson, Ph.D., and Kathy Kwiatkowski, M.S.*

This theory-driven model of IFSP development gives information on best practices in transition, family involvement, and collaboration with agencies. You'll learn valuable strategies to help you improve the quality of special education services to children from birth to 3 years and their families. Three different models—family systems theory, family stress theory, and ecological—show you how to plan and provide early intervention services.

**Catalog No. 7802-Y      $35**

## SELF-TALK
### Communication Boards for Children and Adults
*by Janice A. Johnson, M.S., CCC-SLP*

You can save hours of time spent constructing language boards for nonverbal clients. These five communication boards provide clear, colorful, and appealing pictures on a flexible vinyl-like material. Easily wipe this surface clean for continued use. The vocabularies presented on the boards are developmentally sequenced for early preschoolers through adults.

**Catalog No. 7347-Y     $29.95**

## SELF-TALK STICKERS
*by Janice A. Johnson, M.S., CCC-SLP*

Use these pressure-sensitive pictures as a supplement to your work with clients using augmentative devices. You'll get two sets of 13 full-color sticker sheets and one set of 13 black-and-white sticker sheets—441 different stickers in all! Blank stickers are include on some sheets to use for client's personal photographs or drawings. Use these stickers alone or with *Self-Talk Communication Boards.*     **Catalog No. 7607-Y     $49**

---